Learning with Nature

BIRMINGHAM CITY
University

Please
remember to
return or
renew on time
to avoid fines

Renew/check due dates via
www.bcu.ac.uk/library

Learning with Nature

A **how-to** guide to **inspiring children** through outdoor **games** and **activities**

Marina Robb · Victoria Mew · Anna Richardson

Published by

Green Books
An imprint of UIT Cambridge Ltd
www.greenbooks.co.uk

PO Box 145, Cambridge CB4 1GQ, England
+44 (0) 1223 302 041

First published in 2015, in England

Marina Robb, Victoria Mew and Anna Richardson have asserted their
moral rights under the Copyright, Designs and Patents Act 1988.

Illustrations © 2015 Susan Kelly

Front cover photograph by Will Heap

Photograph credits given on page 202

Design by Mad-i-Creative
www.mad-i-creative.co.uk

ISBN: 978 0 85784 239 8 (paperback)
ISBN: 978 0 85784 238 1 (hardback)
ISBN: 978 0 85784 240 4 (ePub)
ISBN: 978 0 85784 241 1 (pdf)
Also available for Kindle.

10 9 8 7 6 5 4 3 2

Acknowledgements

The content of this book has come from many wide and varied sources. Some of the activities have been developed by us but many others are from indefinite sources, ranging from modern outdoor practices to ancient traditions. Thanks to all those past and present who have inspired the activities in this book.

For their direct support in helping this book come into the world, we send sincere thanks to Duncan McTeer, our patient and generous graphic designer; to Susan Kelly for her wonderful illustrations; to Tim Robb for his hours of spelling and grammar checks; and to Catherine Hooper, who has kindly given her time and advice in the crucial latter stages of writing the book. We thank all those who have contributed to the book and consented to photos being used – Gordon Hillman, Will Heap, Dhyana Miller and Julie Ruse, Dan Puplett and John Scathe – with special thanks to the young people featured, and apologies to anybody whose name we have inadvertently omitted.

We are grateful for the cumulative heritage of previous teachers that have influenced each of us, with warmest thanks to Jon Young and the indigenous teachings that have deeply touched all three of us.

Marina

I thank my father and mother for sharing their openness and welcoming of people from all backgrounds and their energy for life. To my husband, Geoff Robb, for his love and generosity, sisters Alba Lewis and Deborah Lewis, and my children Dylan, Leia and Jake. I particularly thank Stephanie Pugsley, Carmen Ablack, Richard Cleminson and Arwyn Thomas for mentoring and helping me to value myself and follow my dreams. I thank my teachers along the way – Annie Spencer, Dr Malcolm Plant, Don Americo, Martin Prechtel, Victor Sanchez, Salvatore Gencarelle – and work colleagues, all of whom have fostered and inspired my connection with nature. Finally, I would like to thank all the young people I have met through the years who have brought me laughter, challenge and hope.

Anna

Thanks to all the amazing children who have touched my life, especially my son Oran Ash. Thanks to Mat Ash for all his support, extraordinary knowledge and skills that he has shared behind the scenes. To my parents for their unconditional love and help whenever needed. To all the dear friends and family who have been constant guides. To all those who have shared their indigenous lineages of teachings with me – Eliot Cowan, Jon Young, David Wiley, Thomas Shorr-Konn and Graham Johnson. A special thanks to Gordon Hillman, Professor of Archaeobotany, for his tireless generosity and inspiration in sharing his love and knowledge of the plant world and the wild food of our ancestors. To the authors of all the field guides and informative books that have informed me in the absence of direct teachers. To all those who have supported my work over the years, including Circle of Life Rediscovery, Debby and Mark Hunter of Annan Froebel School, Alice Craggs and family at Wowo campsite, River Jones and Ian Dunford at CCE University of Sussex, and Rachel Bennington. A special thanks to Helen Thoms for introducing me to forest school and opening the door to many years of collaborative and magical work together. Thanks to the heart of gold in each and every person, the generosity of the Earth and the great mystery of life.

Victoria

I feel privileged in having had many opportunities throughout my teenage years to experience a plethora of vocational trainings in primitive skills and nature awareness. I send deep thanks to my mum, Jenny Cubitt-Smith, for helping me find my way to these courses, and to both my parents for enabling me to do them, and for their ongoing love and support. I am grateful for the many teachers who inspired and motivated me. Lastly, yet importantly, my gratitude goes to all those who have stewarded wild spaces, however small, that enable this work; especially to those at Plawhatch Farm and Hawthbush Farm for opening their land to our work with young people.

Contents

point of view, that of a naturalist, I sincerely fear for the future of my kind. How can young people learn about nature from the Internet or in libraries? How will that ignite a lifelong interest in the most beautiful things our world has to offer? It won't. Young people need to get out and see nature; hear it, they need to feel it – a newt tickling the palm of their hand, the edge of a feather, the sweetness of a ripe blackberry.

In my lifetime of interest in wildlife, I have witnessed the sad and dramatic decline of many species that as a child I considered 'common': kestrels, skylarks, grey partridges and lapwings, to name a few. But coincidentally, I have also seen a tragic extinction in the UK countryside ... that of the young naturalist. I walk with my dogs twice daily through woods near where I grew up, and in years I have not seen a single child making camps, climbing trees, damming streams, let alone looking for birds' nests, catching grass snakes or tracking foxes. Not one; they have gone.

Well, not gone exactly. They have been imprisoned, protected from the dirty and dangerous outdoors by being locked up inside in front of televisions and computers. Increasingly, they have become fat and bored, they have become allergic to things and less socially competent. These are not opinions, they are facts; a horrible reflection of the mistreatment of generations of young minds and bodies. From my

This book offers a chance to the youth of today and the nature of tomorrow. It has a wealth of structured, tried and tested projects, ideas and games designed to allow children to breathe fresh air and engage personally with a real world where their minds and bodies can develop and bloom, burst into life, and inspire them to love life.

Chris Packham (TV presenter and naturalist)

Over the last few years, the need for encouraging young people to get outdoors has captured the interest of educators, families, researchers and policymakers worldwide. The nature connection movement has gained momentum through such books as Richard Louv's *Last Child in the Woods*, which speaks of an emerging 'nature deficit disorder', referring to the negative consequences of a childhood without sufficient time spent playing and connecting with the natural world. There are now forest schools all over Britain, and increasingly worldwide. We have abundant research telling us that nature is fundamentally beneficial and leads to well-being, health and happiness. Nevertheless, children are rarely allowed to roam outdoors. In a single generation since the 1970s, children's 'radius of activity' – the area around their home where they are allowed to roam unsupervised – has declined by almost 90% (Sanford Gaster, 'Urban Children's Access to their Neighbourhoods', 1991).

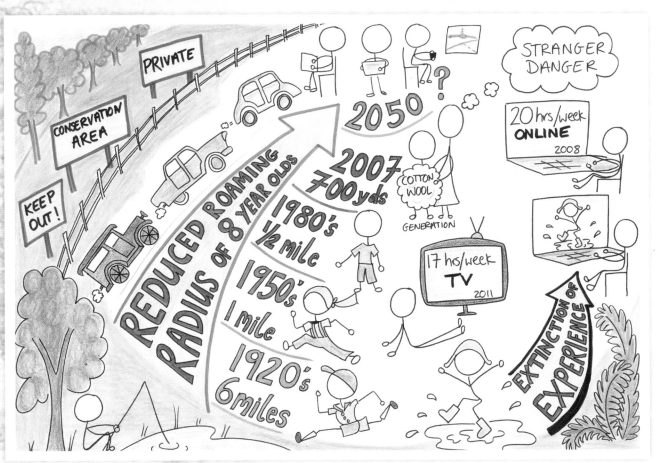

Simply spending time outdoors and interacting with the elements gives our senses a host of stimuli that cannot be recreated indoors. The significant cultural changes towards indoor play and interaction with video games, iPads and television are known to be a threat to healthy development. It is not that technological advances should not be celebrated, but they are addictive and take us away from other pastimes.

For anyone to care for nature, they need to know it; to know it in their bodies, to feel it through their senses. This process begins most naturally in childhood: going outdoors lays critical foundations for a healthy developing brain. Splashing in the mud, making shelters, hiding, pretending and imitating, and exploring the world are all multi-sensory experiences that grow neural pathways and reduce cortisol, which is released in response to stress. When we are stressed, we cannot learn.

Children naturally explore and experiment, whether this is poking around in streams, climbing trees or mixing ingredients. It is part of feeling fully alive. Things can sometimes go wrong. But, statistically, the chance of anything going seriously wrong is vanishingly small, and the risks can be managed through taking a thoughtful, balanced approach. What is more, these adventurous behaviours lead to all kinds of benefits, including hard-wiring the brain, building and maintaining resilience and, in an uncertain world, helping children to manage their choices and grow their capacity to take healthy risks. Tim Gill, one of Britain's leading thinkers on childhood, gives a simple example in an article in The *Guardian* on 3 April 2009:

Climbing a tree – working out how to start, testing for strength, feeling how the breeze in your face also sways the branches underfoot, glimpsing the changing vista through the leaves, dreaming about being king or queen of the jungle, shouting to your friends below once you've got as high as you dare – is an immersive, 360-degree experience that virtual or indoor settings simply cannot compare with.

As parents and teachers, we need to consider how and why we prevent risk-taking, and own our fear so that we do not pass it on to the youth of today.

as the 'art of questioning', developed by Jon Young. There are three levels to the question: the confidence builder, the edge question and beyond-the-edge question. It is a vital approach in this book also. The idea is to join the person in their curiosity with an open mind. It really is an art, however: taking the concept and applying it in an unskilled way can result in others feeling patronised by a 'know-it-all'. To avoid this, find a question you can genuinely develop.

The art of questioning: a mentor's tool

Have you ever been curious about something, perhaps a type of tree, and asked someone what it is? After receiving the answer, 'a silver birch', you are left satisfied and move on. We witness this many times. A direct answer usually results in very little further interest. Igniting a person's authentic curiosity by responding to a question with another question or a descriptive observation is a useful technique known

With an open mind we learn more. A series of questions upon finding a burdock seed head could be: what does this plant depend on for its disposal? If we were to plant some of the seeds, where do you think it would like to grow? The parent plant must have grown from a seed; I wonder where the parent plant is and what kind of journey the seed had to get here?

The more we learn about nature the more we realise there is to learn. Finding your own edge of curiosity enables you to engage and explore something with the person through questions and observations before giving it a name, if the person still wants a label for it. It is like planting a seed – the person's curiosity tells you the ground is fertile. In *Coyote's Guide to Connecting with Nature*, Jon Young describes how we as mentors must get back to the 'beginner's mind' – the mind of humility and fresh discovery. Over the years, this approach instils an open-minded fascination with life, the kind of sparkle you witness in someone who is truly alive.

Naturalist profiles: a learning tool

During any outdoor experience, we come into contact with a variety of species. To maximise learning, it can be satisfying, when back home or in the classroom, to create a naturalist profile of a species that sparked your interest (see opposite). Over time, building up a file or filling a scrapbook becomes a source of pride.

Use field guides, the Internet or other resources to find out more about the plant, animal or mineral and enjoy recording the results in words and drawings. Some helpful headers include: size, life-span, habitat, habits, diet, predators, tracks and scat (droppings).

Burdock (*Arctium lappa*)

Making the most of this book

The games and activities in this book have been tried and tested on a diverse range of groups, from nursery children to adults, and from families to school groups and camps. In many cases, the activities and games can be adapted to cater for a wide range of ages and players. Each game or activity lists a 'how to' section, the relevant resources, variations on the activity, and an insight into the invisible learning that can be gained from a game.

Each page speaks of a way of learning that is timeless, that invites mutual exploration and fun, where the line between adult or teacher and child or learner becomes blurred. The learning appears invisible at times, but occurs none the less.

Before you get going

When working in a woodland, or the outdoors more generally, it is essential to have a clear idea about boundaries and agreements for games or activities. For boundaries, use a landmark or a number of chosen trees. Perhaps decide on an animal sound to signal the end of the game – a wolf howl works well!

In terms of agreements, aim to leave the land better than you found it, taking care of the natural resources. Consider the following before working with a group: tool safety (see pp.82-3), looking after nature (see pp.18-21), foraging wild plants (see p.158), and fire safety (see pp.160-1).

The following pages offer hundreds of inspiring ways to be outdoors that will bring laughter and fun to a walk in the park, woods, garden or playground! It will encourage enthusiasm and understanding about the value of nature through engaging, practical

and useful activities for all ages, forging a heartfelt relationship that will renew and inform our culture, creating love and respect for the natural world.

Looking after nature

Human beings have always had an important role as caretakers of the natural world. Human interaction with natural resources often involves manipulation of nature for our benefit and, at times, we directly use parts of living plants and trees. Indeed, all living things including humans share in the cycle of life and death. This is unavoidable. By developing our relationship with nature through the activities in this book, we begin to interact with nature in a considerate and respectful manner that fosters long-term personal and planetary well-being.

Some of our generation have inherited a way of thinking that says it's OK to exploit natural resources in unsustainable ways. In response to this, some well-intentioned people and organisations tried to over-protect nature, severely limiting what people could do. Neither of these positions – exploitation or protection – has proven successful in developing responsible environmental behaviour in the younger generations. We now know that people need to connect with and learn from nature for a healthy and happy life. We also know that nature flourishes through the tending of the land, water and all its inhabitants.

Our hunter-gatherer ancestors understood the interplay between nature and people. Through caring for the wilds while meeting their own needs, they lived in landscapes that thrived. Examples of this have been found on all seven continents. In California, after the indigenous people were moved to create national parks, the population of oak trees aged and very few young oaks grew. It was discovered that, for generations, the native Californian tribes gathered acorns to process for food, and planted thousands of acorns along their way, resulting in the oak forests of California. Indigenous people around the world surely had extensive knowledge of natural resources that were carefully managed. Today we have much to learn from our roots.

A core principle of the caretaking mindset is to always ensure the regeneration of natural resources. **Our message is: always leave a place better than you found it.**

Caretaking approaches and activities

Fire

It is a good idea to keep fires in one location, as a fire will destroy the seed bank in the soil immediately beneath it. When wandering in woodland, it is essential to first check whether you are allowed to make fires, and then ensure that they are only small.

Small temporary fire

Leave no trace

- Remove all the leaves and sticks to clear a circle about 1.5m wide.
- Make a small fire (see fire lighting, p.178).
- When it is time to go, put out the fire with water. Use a stick to mix the water with the hot sticks to ensure the fire is out. Check this by touching the ash and water to feel it is cold (do so carefully). It is best to wash wet ash off your hands, as it can be alkaline.

- Pick up all cool blackened sticks and charcoal and scatter widely in the surrounding area.
- Try and replicate the layers of the forest by gathering the decomposed leaves and materials from another area and scattering them where the fire was, as the first layer. Cover this layer with the top layer of the forest – usually leaves that have not begun to decompose.
- If done well, any trace of a fire should be undetectable!

Remains of fire

No trace

Other considerations

- While dry dead wood is essential for a fire, leave enough for habitat piles; for long-term sites, consider buying firewood from sustainable forests.
- Always check the subsoil of the ground before making a fire. Underground fires can occur, especially if there are peat soils or conifer tree roots in contact with a fire.
- Never leave a fire unattended.

Trees and plants

Plants are essential to life on Earth as we know it. They provide oxygen, food, shelter, clothing and medicine; they are the only living things able to convert sunshine into food that other life can consume. Plants have their own communities and life cycles within our ecosystem, so it is important to look after them and to harvest with care and respect in a regenerative way (see foraging wild plants p.158).

Caretaking ideas

- Planting trees and wild flowers.
- Pruning and cutting back.
- When gathering plants for tea, see if there are any seeds. If so, collect them! Consider the habitat these plants like – could you grow some?
- If you find berries that birds like, put some on your bird table or feeder. Who knows where the birds will disperse the seeds!

Animals and habitats

For wild animals, survival is a constant challenge. Our impact on their world is far greater than we imagine. It is important to consider this when spending time in nature. Getting outdoors is great, but do not bring indoor habits outside. Can you find signs of what creatures live in this place? How does cold, or lack of rain, affected them? If you take or eat berries, are you leaving enough for the birds and animals?

By asking these kinds of questions, you end up becoming a caretaker, and conservation ideas spring up without any effort.

Caretaking ideas

- Feed animals in the colder months.
- Leave areas of the woods or the garden completely untouched, as havens for wildlife and plants.
- Provide water that is not frozen for birds and animals to drink in winter.
- Leave nest materials on branches or fences, e.g. wool in spring.
- Remove litter and recycle.
- Build a hotel for insects (see p.94).
- Create hedgehog habitats by leaving brush piles.

It is often said that caring for nature, or promoting going outside, is in some way going backwards. On the contrary! Once you get outside, something happens that feels good and does good.

A brush pile for wildlife

Warm-ups

Pattern ball

Stay alert – here comes another one!

Resources:	1–4 balls
Players:	8+
Age:	7+
Duration:	5+ minutes

How to

- Organise the group in a circle.
- Throw the ball to one person, saying their name as you throw. Ask the person who receives the ball to throw it to a different person, saying their name.
- The ball must be thrown to a new person each time until every member of the group has received the ball once, and the ball is returned to the first thrower. Remember the throwing pattern.
- Repeat the same throwing order again, and when the group is ready, add in another ball, following the same pattern.
- Add in up to 4 balls!

Variations

- Reverse the order in which you have been throwing the balls.

Invisible learning

This game is a favourite for helping people learn names and become familiar with a group.

Look up, look down

Who's it going to be?

Resources:	None
Players:	8+
Age:	8+
Duration:	5+ minutes

How to

- Form the group in a circle.
- Explain that they will put their heads down in response to the command 'look down', and will then be asked to 'look up'.
- When they look up, they must look directly at the face of one of the people in the circle.
- If two people are looking directly at each other, they are out.
- Keep going until there are only a few left.

26

Variations

- Encourage people to pull funny faces!

Invisible learning

This activity is really fun and gets people giggling. It helps bond a group and is inclusive.

Animal forms

Learn about animals and birds through moving like them.

Resources:	None
Players:	Any
Age:	Any
Duration:	5+ minutes

How to

- Form the group in a circle.

- Let the group know that you are going to lead some warm-up movements with a twist.

- Share stretches that embody the movement of an animal (in this book 'animal' includes insects and amphibians) or a bird. For example, act like a buzzard ruffling its feathers, by rolling your shoulders back. You could then roll your shoulders forward and be an owl coughing up a pellet, which usually gets some sound effects and laughs.

- Once you have led a few movements, go around the circle inviting ideas from the group.

- There are countless ideas … a back stretch could be a deer rubbing its antlers on a tree. A hip stretch could be a fox going for a wee!

Variations

- Give each person the name of an animal or bird and get them to act it out for the rest of the group to guess what species they are.

Invisible learning

This activity invites playfulness and is a good way to start the day. Players explore with their body how it might feel to have antlers, feathers, or to move as slowly as a stalking cat.

It brings a group together in a shared experience that can feel slightly silly at first, but through moving and stretching it becomes grounding.

Palm tag

Run everyone's energy out!

Resources:	None
Players:	8+
Age:	7+
Duration:	5+ minutes

How to

- Set the boundaries for the game and draw attention to any hazards.

- Everyone must place one hand on their lower back with their palm facing outwards. This is everyone else's target.

- Their other hand is out in front of them with their index finger pointing out. This finger is the only part of their body they can tag people with. Everyone is 'it'.

- Each person must be aware of everyone around them, as creative chaos ensues when everyone is trying to tag everyone else's palm.

- Once tagged, people need to sit down and count to 20 before rejoining the game.

Variations

- When tagged, players remain out of the game – this way you are left with a duel at the end!

Invisible learning

As everyone can tag you, it expands the senses, especially visual awareness. This is a brilliant way to get people warmed up and to release energy in a focused way. It is a fun game in which nobody loses or wins, so it tends not to leave anyone with bad feelings and invites a sense of inclusiveness.

Beetle tag

Watch out – everybody's 'it'!

Resources:	None
Players:	8+
Age:	7+
Duration:	5+ minutes

How to

- Set up this game by telling the group that in a moment, but not quite yet, everybody will be 'it'.
- Establish a boundary for the game.
- Everybody has to tag other people's limbs (arms and legs).
- Use any of your limbs to tag with (softly!).
- If someone else tags one of your limbs, e.g. your left leg, then you 'lose' this leg and must hop on your right. If one of your arms gets tagged, put it behind your back.
- If you lose all your limbs, you become a beetle and lie on your back wiggling your four limbs.
- Other players can free beetles by touching their forehead to bring them back into the game with all limbs intact.
- If two people tag each other's limbs at the same time, they both lose that limb, so be sneaky and catch people off guard.
- You can only tag one limb at a time.

Rose chafer
(*Cetonia aurata*)

Variations

- An alternative to lying on the ground like a beetle is to run and touch a designated nearby tree to revive your limbs and then rejoin the game.

Invisible learning

This is a great activity for a bit of silliness and a good runaround. You need to have your wits about you, as everybody is 'it'. The game heightens agility and highlights awareness.

29

Owls and crows

True or false?

Resources:	2 boundary markers, 10–20 true or false statements
Players:	8+
Age:	7+
Duration:	5+ minutes

How to

- Divide the group into equal-sized teams – one owls, one crows.
- Assemble each team in a straight line facing the other team, about 3m apart.
- Mark out a safe zone behind each team.
- Call out a true or false statement.
- If the answer is true, the crows chase the owls towards the owls' safe zone. If the answer is false, the owls chase the crows.
- If you are tagged before reaching your safe zone, join the opposite team.

- Start with a few easy statements and then increase the complexity as appropriate.
- Example statements:
  'The sun rises in the east.'
  'Acorns grow on hazel trees.'
  'Sycamore seeds are dispersed by wind.'

Carrion crow
(*Corvus corone*)

Variations

- With older or more experienced groups, have volunteers come to the end of the line and create their own true or false statements.

Invisible learning

This activity teaches facts in a fun way and shows where gaps in knowledge occur.

30

Mystery guess

Who nose what creature I'm thinking of?

Resources:	Creature clues
Players:	2+
Age:	4+
Duration:	5+ minutes

How to

- Tell the group that you are going to give them clues about an animal, and they have to guess which one you are thinking about.

- Ask them not say the answer out loud, but to put their finger on their nose to signal they know.

- They might think they know the answer and then another clue will prove them wrong, so they must quickly take their finger off their nose or pretend they were just scratching it!

Variations

- Once you've got the hang of it, let someone else have a go at thinking of a creature and making up the clues.

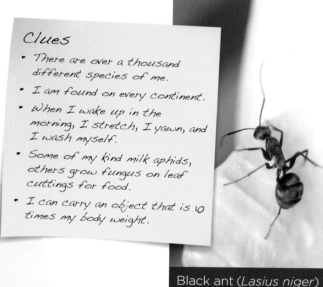

Clues

- There are over a thousand different species of me.
- I am found on every continent.
- When I wake up in the morning, I stretch, I yawn, and I wash myself.
- Some of my kind milk aphids, others grow fungus on leaf cuttings for food.
- I can carry an object that is 10 times my body weight.

Black ant (*Lasius niger*)

Invisible learning

This is a fun way to teach facts about creatures and can be a great way to introduce an activity that involves the creature you are describing. It often elicits a response of 'Wow! A peregrine falcon is the fastest creature on Earth? They can reach a speed of 200mph!'

This activity also gets you questioning what you think you know about familiar creatures, e.g. many people assume that a male blackbird's beak is black, but it is orangey-yellow.

What am I?

Ask questions to discover what you are.

Resources:	Stickers with nature names written or drawn on
Players:	2+
Age:	5+
Duration:	5+ minutes

How to

- Everyone gets a sticker put on them in a place where they cannot read it (on their forehead or back). On each sticker is the name or drawing of an animal or plant, e.g. a rabbit.

- Find out what you are by asking questions that have a 'yes' or 'no' answer.

- Help other people find out what they are by answering their questions if you know the answer.

Variations

- Play in pairs without stickers, with one person thinking of an animal or plant and the other person asking questions to find out what it is.

- Try nature charades, where you act out an animal and others guess what you are.

Rabbit
- Do I eat meat? No
- Do I build a nest? No
- Do I make my home in the ground? Yes
- Do I come out in the night? No
- Am I bigger than a mouse? Yes
- Do foxes eat me? Yes
- Am I a rabbit? Yes

Common rabbit (*Oryctolagus cuniculus*)

Invisible learning

This is a great way to break the ice and get a group mingling. Players learn more about animals, birds, insects and plants, and they learn to work together as they pool their knowledge to answer questions.

Nature names

Create a connection to a specific species in seconds.

Resources:	Paper with nature names
Players:	Any
Age:	Any
Duration:	5+ minutes

How to

- For each person in the group, write down the name of one plant, animal or bird from your ecological neighbourhood.
- Put the names in a bowl and ask the participants to pick out a name. This will be their 'nature name' for the day, week, etc.
- Ask each person to find out something about their name and share it with the group. They can use their knowledge, field guides or the Internet at home. Find out where it lives, how long it lives, how big it grows and whether you can eat it?
- Get each person to draw their species.

Variations

- What sounds or movements do the animals and birds make? Play a 'guess what my nature-name is' game using sounds or movements.
- Ask the group to make their own list of species. This can be quite revealing and interesting.

Invisible learning

Nature names provides a direct way of engaging with your environment and helps you to remember details that otherwise might escape you!

By introducing lots of different ways of paying attention to nature, before you know it, you understand a lot more about your surroundings and the species that share it with you.

33

Plants and trees

Plant duplication

Learn how to recognise different plants.

Resources:	Bandanas, plants or tree leaves
Players:	2–30
Age:	4+
Duration:	10+ minutes

How to

- Collect leaves from 5 to 9 trees or plants in the immediate area.
- Arrange them on a bandana and cover them with a second bandana.
- Set the boundaries of the game, determining how far players can go.
- State that everything hidden under the bandana was collected from within those boundaries.
- Ask the players to get into pairs or small groups.
- Reveal the leaves and give the players 15 seconds to look at them. Then, cover the leaves again.
- Send the players off to gather one of each of the leaves and return with them as quickly as possible.
- If the players struggle, allow them a second look at the leaves.

Variations

- Give each group a bandana on which to arrange the leaves in the original order.
- Have a second game using other parts from the same plants or trees (seeds, catkins, flowers).
- Once everyone is back with their leaves, gather in a circle and discuss the names of the species. You can even play the memory game by removing one leaf and getting the players to note which one is missing.

Invisible learning

An excellent activity to raise interest in plants through the guise of a challenge. By searching for specific leaves, the players will have to look high and low to find the same leaf shapes. This develops a 'search image' in their mind.

Select this activity as a preliminary game using the plants you will go on to forage for.

Go on to look more closely at the leaves they got wrong to understand the differences. This helps build up tree and plant identification skills.

You're only safe if...

A great 'tag' game to find out what's out there and to keep you active!

Resources:	None
Players:	2–30
Age:	3+
Duration:	10+ minutes

How to

- Set a clear boundary for the game, depending on age and how well you know the group.
- Choose 4 to 6 species of plants or trees that are within the boundary.
- Bring the players to each plant in turn and get them to call out which species they are touching.
- To start play, shout out the name of a tree or plant. Each player must run to that species without getting tagged by the leader – as soon as they touch it they are 'safe'
- If a player is tagged, they join the leader and help chase the other players.
- The game is over when everyone is tagged.

Variations

- Instead of using 4-6 plants, use different themes or situations instead. E.g. not touching the ground; touching something red, etc.
- Try it in a different natural space, or in a playground.

Invisible learning

This is a fantastic way to burn off energy while learning to identify plants and trees and remember their names.

This activity is useful to prime a session on foraging so that children can recognise the plants or trees before starting to learn their uses.

Blindfolded recognition

This improves plant and tree recognition, and stimulates awareness, seeing with new eyes.

Resources:	Bandanas, plant or tree leaves
Players:	1–16
Age:	4+
Duration:	20+ minutes

How to

- Arrange the players in a circle and blindfold them or ask them to close their eyes.

- Give each person a different type of leaf. This is their leaf number 1. Ask them to touch it, smell it and get to know it. Does it have a particular shape? Is it soft or spiky? Ask them not to name it!

- After a short while, ask each player to pass their leaf to the person on their left.

- Repeat the process 3 times in total. Number the leaves 1, 2 and 3.

- Place all the leaves on a cloth or bandana in the centre of the circle.

- Ask participants to remove their blindfolds and see if they can find their leaf 1. Ask them how they identified it. Repeat with leaves 2 and 3.

Variations

- Get participants to describe what they are touching as they explore their leaf.

- Put players in pairs in the last part of the game. One player describes the leaf while the other has to pick out the correct leaf.

- Let the players feel a different leaf each, then put all the leaves in a mystery bag and see if they can find their own leaf just by touching.

- Once they have found their leaf, send them on a mission to find the plant or tree the leaf came from.

Invisible learning

By inhibiting sight, players develop their other senses more as they explore their leaves.

It makes looking for the leaves' identifying characteristics fun and challenging, and builds a deeper relationship with the plant or tree.

Players will never look at a leaf in the same way again! They are also likely to be able to recognise it and name it, and remember its characteristics.

Leaf puzzles

Have fun working out how a leaf fits together!

Resources:	Safe large leaves
Players:	2+
Age:	2+
Duration:	10+ minutes

How to

- Take a large plant or tree leaf from a plentiful area, e.g. burdock, dock, sycamore (nothing poisonous).
- Break it up into pieces.
- Ask participants to put it back together.

Variations

- Can be played individually or as a team challenge.
- Use leaves as money to play shops, e.g. oak leaves = 10p, hazel leaves = 5p.
- Vary the level of the challenge by the number of pieces you rip the leaf into.

Invisible learning

This is a problem-solving activity that teaches about a particular plant or tree. It requires the player to look carefully at the leaf, feel it, and, without knowing, note the shape and the uniqueness of the leaf. One of the most helpful parts of the leaf to look at when completing the jigsaw are the veins, and also how the two sides of the leaf differ. This activity can improve team work.

Meet a tree

Getting to know a tree in an unforgettable way!

Resources:	Blindfolds, trees
Players:	2–30
Age:	6+
Duration:	20+ minutes

How to

- Ask the group to get into pairs: one is A, one is B.
- A puts on a blindfold.
- B turns A around to disorient them and carefully leads A to a tree in the nearby area.
- Let A explore the tree. Does the bark feel rough? Can you feel the roots? How large is the trunk? Are there any branches you can reach? Is there any moss growing on the tree? We encourage you to do this bit in silence, so B steps back.
- When A has investigated his or her tree enough, B gently leads A back to where you started.
- Before taking off the blindfold, ask A to imagine what the tree looks like.
- Now is the time for A to find the tree. Depending on the age group and purpose of the activity, let A find his or her tree independently. If A needs help, B can say when he or she is getting warmer or cooler.
- Celebrate the moment of recognition.
- Swap over to give B a go.

Variations

- Narrow or expand your boundaries to make success easier or to really challenge yourselves.
- If you cannot find your tree, so be it! For those who struggle to find their tree, they can experience strong emotions, so leave time for reflection.

Invisible learning

This game provides lots of learning opportunities. It engages individuals with many aspects of tree identification while building trust between the players and challenging them to use their non-dominant senses. The use of blindfolds can make individuals feel vulnerable, so the rewards of succeeding often feel greater.

Scavenger hunt

Find out more about what is around you.

Scavenger Hunt

1. A feather
2. Something that's been eaten
3. Something that's yellow
4. Something that smells
5. Something that's rough
6. A seed
7. Something that comes from an animal

Resources:	Scavenger hunt list
Players:	1–30
Age:	3+
Duration:	20+ minutes

How to

- Play individually, in pairs or in small groups.
- Each group is given a pre-prepared list of objects to find at the site (see examples above).
- Send the groups out to see what they can find in a set period of time.
- Celebrate and share what they have found.

Variations

- Send different groups out in different directions to get to know the lie of the land, introducing the concept of north, south, east and west.
- Rather than gathering the objects, ask them to draw them, e.g. a blue flower, a deer track.
- Set up the game as a series of challenges – the adult has the list, but the players are only told the next item when they have found the one before.
- Use artistic licence to create a magical, imaginative scavenger hunt that can lead to storytelling activities and free play. For example, find something which could be an elf's hat, a gnome's beard, a giant's ear or a fairy's wing.

Invisible learning

This is an effective game to familiarise players with their environment. It gets everyone exploring while engaged on a mission, cultivating curiosity about nature and the story of a place. It introduces such themes as identification, sensory awareness and ecology. It opens up inquisitive minds and sharpens observation skills.

Reflective questions

- What other creatures live here?
- What signs would they leave behind them?
- Where would we find them?
- What do they eat and who or what eats them?

Camera kids

Isn't nature amazing? So much to see!

Resources:	None
Players:	2–30
Age:	4+
Duration:	15+ minutes

How to

- Get the group into pairs and decide who in each pair will be the photographer and who will be the camera.
- Explain how the camera works: when you touch an earlobe, the camera shutter closes (i.e. the player closes his or her eyes). When you touch the earlobe again, the player opens their eyes. Say 'click' to take the photo.
- Once the group has got the idea, they can go off and photograph the 3 most beautiful images they can find.
- The photographer keeps the camera shutter closed until he/she arrives at an image, then open the shutter and take a picture.
- Invite the players to keep quiet on the journey.
- Get the pairs to swap over.

Variations

- After returning, hand out paper and pens, and ask them to draw the photograph they liked best. Gather as a group and share the images.
- For regular visits to the same spot, establish a routine of taking a photo at the same place through the seasons to see how it changes.

Invisible learning

This activity invites awe and wonder and allows players to see different parts of nature from many perspectives. It builds trust and respect between partners, and it is important to emphasise the need to look after your 'camera' when the shutter is closed. It is a fun way to explore or compare a new landscape, or to see a familiar landscape with fresh eyes.

Animals and birds

Sleeping fawn

Feel so at home outdoors that you snuggle into the leaves...

Fallow deer fawn (*Dama dama*)

Resources:	None
Players:	4+
Age:	3+
Duration:	5+ minutes

How to

- Tell the group a short story about how fawns (young deer) do not have a strong scent, and when their mothers leave them to go and feed, their survival depends on staying still so predators do not see them (as they cannot smell them).

- Tell them that in a moment they will become a fawn and go a short distance into the surrounding area to find a place to sleep.

- Soon there will be predators – foxes, large cats, wolves – coming to look for their dinner! They will try to make the sleeping fawns move or laugh by roaming among them and may even sniff them (predators may not physically touch sleeping fawns).

- If a sleeping fawn moves or giggles, they become a predator.

- After a short while there will be more predators than sleeping fawns, so either continue until all have changed role or end the game with some surviving fawns.

Variations

- This game is a good precursor to wildcats prowling (see p.65).

- As the first predator, prowl a little further from the participants at the beginning, giving them a prolonged period of still and quiet while they soak up the landscape.

- This can be great to play shortly after lunch if there is a lull of energy, as it can facilitate a siesta!

Invisible learning

This activity introduces knowledge about local animals and provides an opportunity for stillness.

Over time, it can help build up children's relationship with the core routine of sit spot (see p.92). Ask the children questions, such as, what did you hear when you were a sleeping fawn? Was your sleeping space comfortable?

Otter, salmon, mosquito

A lively team game to show what eats what!

Resources:	None
Players:	6+
Age:	6+
Duration:	5+ minutes

How to

- Divide the group into two teams.
- A line is drawn at either end of a defined space ('pitch' shape) of about 10m.
- Ask the group to come up with movements that symbolise an otter, a salmon and a mosquito.
- Explain which animal eats the other animal: otter eats salmon, salmon eats mosquito, mosquito bites otter.
- The game begins with each team deciding which animal to be.
- Both teams stand in a line facing each other, in the middle of the 'pitch'. Start with hands stretched out and fingertips meeting.
- On the count of three, both teams simultaneously reveal which animal they are by doing the relevant movement and saying the animal's name.

- If one team is the otter and the other the mosquito, the mosquitoes chase the otters to their line, trying to catch as many as possible. Whoever is caught becomes part of the other team. Then start again.
- It is a good idea to get the teams to come up with a back-up choice in case they have both chosen the same animal.

Variations

- Choose different ecosystems, food chains and animals.
- Change the size of the space to make it work for all ages.

Invisible learning

A fast moving team game that teaches about food chains and ecosystems in a fun way.

Nest robbers

Become birds and immerse yourself in their world.

Resources: Nest-making material, 'food' objects
Players: 10+
Age: 6+
Duration: 10+ minutes

How to

- Everyone has a role. Initially, most will be songbirds, although a few will be corvids (e.g. crows and ravens) (this could be the adults).
- Players are not allowed to speak during the game; they may only make bird sounds, e.g. squawks and cheeps.
- The songbirds must pair up and build a nest, which they then hide within the delineated playing area.
- In the centre of the playing area is an abundance of 'food' (wrapped sweets or something natural like spruce cones).
- The songbirds must try to get as much food as possible to their nests without a corvid finding them.
- Corvids must try to find the nests and steal food from them.

- Songbirds may only take one piece of food at a time. Corvids may also only steal one piece of food at a time.
- If a corvid tags a songbird holding a piece of food, the food must be returned to the central feeding area.

Variations

- Add in a sparrowhawk who hunts the songbirds. Songbirds are safe from the sparrowhawk when they are touching an oak tree, for example.

Jay (*Garrulus glandarius*)

Invisible learning

This activity exemplifies the life of birds and how they interconnect, as well as the food chains at play and the language birds use to stay safe.

After playing the game, it is good fun to go on a tour of where the pairs hid their nests and bring in aspects about camouflage. Remember to ask the players how they found it in different roles and whether they learned anything about birds.

Run, rabbit, run

When rabbits graze in the meadow, they must be alert at all times, as danger lurks on the edges!

Resources: None
Players: 8+
Age: 6+
Duration: 10+ minutes

How to

- Ask for a volunteer fox. All other players are rabbits.

- To identify foxes and rabbits, foxes hold one hand behind them for their tail and rabbits hold two fingers behind their heads for ears.

- In an open setting (e.g. a meadow), players place bags or an item of clothing within a designated area, to represent burrows. In a woodland setting, specific trees can represent burrows.

- When rabbits are touching the burrow, they are safe from the fox.

- The fox can sneak off somewhere while the rabbits sit or move about, always keeping an eye and ear out for the fox.

- The fox comes out and hunts the rabbits. When rabbits are tagged, they become foxes. The rabbits are safe in their burrows but must not stay there longer than 10 seconds, with the agreement that

the fox will not guard the burrow.

- When all the rabbits have become foxes, the game is over.

Variations

- Consider the behaviour, movements and dominant senses of foxes and rabbits before playing. Rabbits warn their companions of danger by thumping their back paws on the ground.

Common rabbit
(*Oryctolagus cuniculus*)

Invisible learning

This activity promotes an understanding of predator–prey relationships. It creates a need for heightened sensory awareness and increases agility and reflexes. Taking on the roles of the animals and trying out some of their habits fosters empathy with animals.

Eagle eye

Disappear from view in seconds!

Resources:	None
Players:	3+
Age:	4+
Duration:	10+ minutes

How to

- Choose a location that has good cover for hiding. Gather the group here, as this will be the 'eagle's nest'.

- To begin with, the adult takes the role of the eagle at the nest, and the children are mice. The mice are given boundaries and then go and hide.

- The eagle says loudly, 'Eagle's eyes are closing for 30 seconds', then 'Eagle's eyes are opening', closing and opening their eyes accordingly. The eagle scans around for mice. If any are spotted, they must come to the nest!

- The mice must slowly find their way to the eagle's nest. While the eagle closes his or her eyes, the mice must find a new hiding place closer to the eagle's nest.

- The eagle closes their eyes for less time each turn.

- When all the mice have been seen, the game is over.

Variations

- As well as limiting the amount of time the eagle closes their eyes, reduce the length of time the eagle can hunt for mice, e.g. eyes closed for 10 seconds, open for 10 seconds.

Invisible learning

A brilliant game for those who think that being out in nature is too dirty or for those who are worried about creepy crawlies! The game distracts players from these concerns, and soon enough everyone is diving into the undergrowth before the eagle opens their eyes. Players often come back with stories of seeing beetles, spiders and even unfurling ferns. It is an all-time favourite game.

47

Fox and rabbit

Watch out! Where's the fox now?

Resources: None
Players: 8+
Age: 10+
Duration: 5+ minutes

How to

- Ask the group to get into pairs, with one person leading the game.
- Ask for two volunteers – one to be the fox and the other the rabbit.
- Define the boundaries of the game (you will need quite a lot of space).
- Get the pairs to stand in different locations, scattered around the space.
- The fox must catch the rabbit. The only time the rabbit is safe is when he or she hooks on to one of the pairs.
- When a rabbit hooks on to a pair, the partner furthest from the rabbit becomes the rabbit and must run to save his or her life.

- If the fox catches the rabbit before he or she can hook on to one of the pairs, the players swap roles and the rabbit becomes the fox and chases the rabbit who was a fox just a moment beforehand.
- This is a fast-moving game – the role swaps can be swift and you need to keep alert. Have a couple of trial runs to see how it works before you begin!

Red fox (*Vulpes vulpes*)

Variations

- Replace the fox and rabbit with other predator–prey relationships.

Invisible learning

This is a high-energy game. Players must pay attention to what is going on and often observe and develop strategies, e.g. use less energy than others.

Bat and moth

Track down your prey by sound.

Resources:	Blindfold
Players:	8+
Age:	6+
Duration:	5+ minutes

Common pipistrelle
(*Pipistrellus pipistrellus*)

How to

- Form the group in a circle and ask for a volunteer to be the bat and another to be the moth.

- The rest of the group becomes the 'cave wall', while you blindfold the bat.

- Get the bat and moth each to make up a call for themselves – keep the sounds simple.

- The bat has to catch the moth, using sound rather than sight. Every time the bat calls, the moth must reply immediately.

- The players forming the 'cave wall' must also make a sound back to the bat, if he/she calls while close to the wall.

- Depending on the age and size of the group, introduce more moths and/or more bats.

Variations

- Introduce another predator, e.g. an owl, to eat the bat. Do this by blindfolding the owl and allowing it to move one step only when it hears the bat sound.

Invisible learning

This activity introduces the idea of predator-prey relationships. It allows the players to rely on what they can hear, trust their instincts and listen carefully. It encourages agility and body confidence, and is a great starter for using blindfolds.

Owls and mice

Quiet, little mouse. Don't make a sound!

Resources:	Berries and nuts, bowl, bandana
Players:	6+
Age:	5+
Duration:	10+ minutes

How to

- **Note any allergies within the group.**
- Ask for a volunteer to be an owl, and blindfold him or her.
- The rest of the group are the mice.
- Put out feeding bowls filled with berries and nuts. You'll need a bowl for each mouse.
- The mice are allowed to take just one nut or berry per bowl before they crawl to another bowl. They must keep moving.
- The blindfolded owl is placed among the mice. If the owl hears a mouse, he or she points in that direction. If correct, the mouse is out of the game.
- The adult must discern whether it is an accurate hit.
- The owl is then moved to where the mouse was before being caught.
- The mice must stay alive for as long as possible.

Variations

- If the owl starts pointing everywhere, give the owl 3 misses before changing him or her into a mouse, and asking a new owl to take over.
- Introduce two owls or another mouse predator.

Wood mouse (*Apodemus sylvaticus*)

Invisible learning

This teaches that owls are not only able to see very well, but are also excellent listeners. Their ears are hidden behind a face full of feathers that extend from the top of their head to below the beak. They can hear a mouse moving under a foot of snow, and are known as the silent hunters.

It also shows the perspective of the mice: how they move, what they eat and what eats them.

Otter steals fish

This game shows how a heron will fish patiently for hours, and how otters love a good fish whenever they can get one!

Resources:	Bandana
Players:	8+
Age:	8+
Duration:	5+ minutes

How to

- Get a volunteer to be a heron. He or she will stand over a bandana – the 'fish' – to guard it.
- The others are otters who must try to steal that fish.
- Set a perimeter circle around the heron and his or her fish of about 3m to 5m.
- Make sure that all the otters stand outside this perimeter (it can be helpful to mark this with backpacks or small sticks).
- All at once, the otters must try to take the fish from the ground the heron is guarding.
- An otter is only successful if he or she picks up the fish and takes it out of the perimeter without being tagged by the heron.
- The heron protects the fish by tagging any otters with a light touch. Once tagged, an otter must go back outside the perimeter and try again.
- The heron must not touch the fish at any time.

Variations

- Try with 2 herons.
- When tagged, otters freeze. If they are tagged again, they are unfrozen and can try once more.

Otter (*Lutra lutra*)

Invisible learning

The heron and otters expand the players' visual and auditory awareness. The heron must be aware of all directions at once to protect the fish. The otters must be watching the heron as well as the other otters to find an opportunistic moment to steal the fish.

This is an excellent game to raise the energy (or body temperature) of a group. It is great watching as the players become increasingly confident in risk-taking.

51

Badger nose best

Use essential oils to sniff your way to success!

Resources:	Essential oils, blindfolds
Players:	6+
Age:	8+
Duration:	15+ minutes

How to

- Choose a number of strong-smelling, safe essential oils, e.g. peppermint, lavender or tea tree. **Caution: children must not get oil in their eyes.**
- Before your group arrives, set up a number of scent trails in different directions, one per small group. Drip a few drops on to trees or stones to make a scent trail.
- At the end of the trail, bury a potato a little under the soil. Then put some oil onto a stick and place upright in the ground where the potato is.
- Explain to the groups that badgers are largely nocturnal and don't see very well but can rely on their superb sense of smell to find food.
- The teams must follow the trail, blindfolded, then dig up the potato and get back to the beginning again.
- The teams wait behind an imaginary line, where they are blindfolded, and off they go! The teams are not allowed to dig up the potato until all team members have arrived at the stick.
- The first team back wins!

Variations

- Use this activity to practise mimicking animals' movements – in this case the badger's pacing.
- Use camouflage – chalk for white and charcoal for black – to paint the players' faces so they resemble badgers.

Badger (*Meles meles*)

Invisible learning

This activity puts children in touch with their sense of smell and lets them experience how a badger seeks its food. It provides good team-building opportunities and helps the players to explore different methods of communication. Any blindfolded activity is challenging and opens up the senses.

Badger fact

A badger's sense of smell is 700 to 800 times stronger than ours – wonder what the badger will make of our trail? Pooey!

Master tracker

Who has the eyes of a detective?

Resources: Any object
Players: 8+
Age: 7+
Duration: 10+ minutes

How to

- Get the group into a circle at least 5 paces in diameter. Pick an area that has not been walked on recently to make the circle.

- Throw an object into the middle of the circle – you could use keys.

- Ask for a volunteer to be the detective. The detective's role is to track whoever takes the object by looking for their footprints in the terrain. Send the detective off a short distance and tell them not to look.

- Choose one person to walk normally into the circle, pick up the object, walk back out and put the object in his or her pocket.

- Call the detective back, encourage him or her to walk around the circle and look for signs of disturbance and possibly footprints.

- The detective gets 3 guesses as to who took the object.

- Change roles to give others a go and play again.

Variations

- Discuss what clues you are looking for to detect disturbances, e.g. grass bent in one direction, some grass still slowly springing back, shiny or dull areas depending on recent weather.

Invisible learning

This is a fantastic activity to develop tracking skills in a fun manner and to encourage children to see in a different way. For the person who took the object and for the rest of the group, there is an element of deception so as not to give the 'thief' away.

This activity is challenging but engages keen observation. Through playing it repeatedly, all involved start to build up brain patterns of what the subtle differences in the terrain look like when the ground has been stepped upon. Once your eyes learn to read these differences, the natural world becomes alive in a whole new way.

Wolves and deer

Wolves work together to hunt in packs. Deer use stealth and skill to stay alive. Can you?

Resources: None
Players: 6+
Age: 6+
Duration: 15+ minutes

How to

- Set a clear boundary and remind participants of any hazards.

- Split the group into wolves and deer (with 1 wolf per 5 deer).

- Remind the group about the behaviour of deer and wolves and ask them to use the skills of fox walking, owl eyes and deer ears (see pp.57-69). Discuss briefly the predator–prey relationship.

- Agree on a call back if for any reason the game needs to end early.

- The wolves count to 30 (longer if appropriate) while the deer run and hide.

- The wolves begin the hunt. If they touch a deer, the deer joins the predatory wolf team and hunts down the other deer until they are all caught.

Variations

- The game can become all about chasing but it can be set up to develop camouflage skills and stealth movement.

Fallow deer (*Dama dama*)

Grey wolf (*Canis lupus*)

Invisible learning

This is one of the best ways to get young people, especially teenagers, to stay still and quiet in the natural world. When the deer are waiting to be found, their hearts start beating and they experience what it would be like to be hiding as if their lives depended on it. The moment of whether to run or stay ... Will they be seen? It is simply exhilarating!

The game gives a lot of opportunities to note an individual's strengths in stealth, awareness, camouflage, agility and teamwork.

It can be valuable to ask some reflective questions after the game: how it felt to be a deer hiding, how it felt to be a wolf, and how different it felt with a bigger wolf pack working together?

Wildlife is watching

How many eyes are watching us right now?

- If you have camouflaged team B well, team A may not find everyone, so take them through again. On a final walk through, have team B slowly rise out of their hiding places to reveal themselves.
- Swap groups over and play again.

Water vole
(*Arvicola amphibius*)

Resources:	None (optional camouflage)
Players:	4–16
Age:	5+
Duration:	10+ minutes

How to

- Inspire the group with a story about camouflage, explaining that wild animals often see us before we see them.
- Split the group into two teams: A and B.
- Team A prepares by playing deer stalk (see p.64).
- Take team B to hide along a small path that has good ground cover.
- Tell team B players to each find a hiding place near the path, where you will help them blend in with their surroundings. They must stay still and quiet as a mouse.
- When ready, call team A to the start of the path.
- Ask team A to fox walk (see p.57) along the path, tell them not to point out people they see, but to keep a tally of those they spot.

Variations

- An effective way to inspire a group is to have a camouflaged adult in the area before the group arrives so they can see how well it works.

Invisible learning

By being still and quiet, players experience nature close up. Sometimes they even see a mouse or songbird coming close to them.

This activity can make the children feel like a prey or predator animal.

Sensory awareness

Fox walking

Silence your movements.

Resources:	None
Players:	1–30
Age:	3+
Duration:	5+ minutes

When foxes are walking, they can freeze in an instant so as not to be noticed. They are able to do this because their balance is so good – from their tracks you can see that their feet stay very close to a central line. When they are hunting, they move by feeling the ground beneath each foot before committing their weight. This enables them to be very quiet and get close to their prey. We can learn from foxes so we can get close to animals in the wild.

How to

- If it's safe, this game is best played barefoot.

- Everyone places their hands over their ears and walks around the space you are in. After a couple of minutes, ask the group to make a circle and share what they noticed. It is likely that someone will say they heard a pounding in their ears or a stomping sound, or that they could feel their whole body jarring with each step they took.

- Show the group how our normal way of walking is a 'controlled fall', in that we have already committed our weight to the step before we have made contact with the ground.

- Invite the group to try moving in a new way.

- First put your weight on one foot and slowly lift the other off the ground. Then bring the other knee up higher than usual and let the foot hang and relax.

- As you lower the foot to meet the ground in front of you, place your foot in the way it naturally moulds to the ground. Only when the foot is placed should you move your weight on to it. Demonstrate this and invite everyone to try it.

- Ask the players to explain out loud the differences between the two ways of walking.

Invisible learning

This is a great way of starting to feel and understand the way animals and birds experience the world, taking us away from our minds and into our senses.

If we use fox walking in wild spaces, we decrease the disturbance we cause and therefore increase our chances of getting close to wildlife.

Owl eyes

Expand your field of vision.

Resources:	None
Players:	1–30
Age:	3+
Duration:	5+ minutes

This exercise enables peripheral vision.

How to

- Form a circle, leaving enough space for people's arms to stretch out.
- Imagine you are owls, which cannot move their eyes inside their head, and fix your eyes on a spot in the distance straight ahead of you.
- Put your arms out in front of you and start wiggling your fingers.
- Slowly separate your arms, moving them out to the sides while keeping your arms straight.
- Notice when your fingers disappear from your sight.

Barn owl (*Tyto alba*)

Invisible learning

So much of our time is spent focusing on things that are in close proximity to us, such as books, television and even just the indoor environment. Using owl eyes opens up peripheral vision, and doing this on a regular basis keeps our eyes healthy while vastly expanding awareness. Looking with owl eyes, we notice subtle movements that also help us to see animals in the wild, perhaps even before they see us.

Deer ears

Amplify your hearing.

Roe deer (*Capreolus capreolus*)

Resources:	None
Players:	1–30
Age:	3+
Duration:	5+ minutes

Deer have evolved over thousands of years as a prey species. They used to have many predators in the UK and so adapted ways to detect approaching dangers and escape. Their acute sense of hearing is one of their main survival attributes.

How to

- Deer use their large, moveable, external ears to pinpoint where sounds are coming from.

- Cup your hands around your ears and see if it amplifies sounds. Now try cupping your hands the other way and note what you can hear.

- By angling their ears the right way, deer can amplify a sound from a particular direction and can help locate birds and animals.

- For beginners, demonstrate deer ears while sitting around the camp fire – the sound of the fire is a great sound to practise deer ears with.

Bring all your animal senses together

'Fox walk' (see p. 57) out to a spot in nature and sit on your own for 5 to 20 minutes. Use your owl eyes and deer ears to experience nature when you are quiet and still. Going to a sit spot (see pp.92-93) offers the closest encounters with animals!

Sense meditation

Lose your mind and come to your senses!

Resources: None
Players: 1–30
Age: 6+
Duration: 5+ minutes

How to

- Invite the group to close their eyes and get comfortable either standing or sitting. Ask them to notice which part of their body is in contact with the ground.

- Ask them to consider what their skin feels like, whether they can feel a breeze, which way the breeze is coming from, if they can sense any moisture in the air.

- Bring their attention to what they are hearing. What is the furthest sound their ears can pick up? What is the closest sound they can hear? What is the loudest sound and the quietest? Is there a direction from which they can't hear a sound?

- Focus on whether they can smell anything in the air. As the sense of smell is closely linked to the sense of taste, invite them to open their lips and sip the air too. While drawing their attention to their sense of taste, ask them if they notice whether they are thirsty.

- Remind them of the other senses they just explored. Holding an awareness of all of these at once, invite them to open their eyes with a soft gaze or owl eyes, as if it is the first time they have seen this place.

Variations

- Go through the senses in a different order.

Invisible learning

Such a simple sense meditation brings the gift of being fully present. A sense meditation is a brilliant way to become physically aware of your surroundings, and is good to do when visiting new places. By paying attention to each of the senses and expanding them, we remind ourselves how much information they bring us that we are often unaware of.

Mystery object

Discover what your senses can tell you ... let your hands be detectives.

Resources: Bag or bandanas, nature objects (1 per person)
Players: 2–16
Age: 2+
Duration: 10+ minutes

How to

- Sit the players in a circle, blindfold them, then hide an object under a bandana in front of them.
- Ask the group not to look under the bandanas.
- In turn, ask each player to feel their object (without looking!) and describe to the group what they feel.
- If they are struggling to describe it, prompt them with questions such as 'Is it warm/spiky/soft?'
- Ask whether any of them have guessed what the object in front of them is.
- Once everyone has had a turn, let them move to feel another object.
- Reveal what is under the bandanas and see if any players have questions about the objects, such as 'What tree is the leaf from?'

Variations

- Put objects in a bag and pass it around the circle.
- Play as a team.
- Sit the players in a circle, blindfold them and put an object in each person's hands. Encourage them to explore the object before you make a sound signal to tell them to pass it to their left and receive a new object.

Invisible learning

Taking the sense of sight away makes space to really explore things with our other senses. This is a good opportunity to practise descriptive words. It is also great for getting people to ask questions about the objects you have chosen. For example, you may include two different types of seed, say burdock seed heads and sycamore seeds, each of which relies on different methods of dispersal.

Nutty squirrels

Who will be the last squirrel standing?

Resources:	Blindfolds, socks, rope (optional)
Players:	6–30
Age:	8+
Duration:	20+ minutes

How to

- Make a wide circle with a boundary (a rope or backpacks work well), at least 8 adult paces in diameter.

- Ask the group to get into pairs: one will be the parent squirrel, one the baby. Give each pair a blindfold and two rolled up socks for their 'nuts'!

- The aim of the game is to get the other squirrels out by throwing nuts at them. The catch is that only the baby can throw nuts and the baby is blindfolded!

- The parent squirrel uses only touch signals on the baby's back to indicate the direction in which to throw nuts at the other squirrels.

- Each baby squirrel starts with 2 nuts, and once these have been thrown there will be plenty on the ground, so the parent squirrel must guide the baby to find and pick up other nuts.

- If a baby squirrel is hit by a nut then the pair is out and forms part of the boundary to watch the game.

- If a parent squirrel is hit, he or she must leave the blindfolded baby to fend for themselves, using their senses to find nuts and target other squirrels. The parent cannot rejoin the game.

Variations

- Communication strategies can be advanced to sound signals alone, in which case the parent squirrel stays on the boundary of the circle for the whole game and uses sound signals to direct the baby squirrel.

Invisible learning

This activity builds trust between players. Tension mounts and concentration intensifies as parent squirrels try to get their babies to understand what they are communicating. It heightens awareness, as everybody must sense and listen in all directions.

Wolf-pack territory

Use your nose to find the boundaries of your pack's territory!

Resources: Essential oils
Players: 9+
Age: 7+
Duration: 15+ minutes

How to

- Gather a range of safe essential oils (lemongrass, peppermint, lavender...) and/or wild leaves. **Caution: oil must not go in eyes.** Good, safe wild leaves to crush and use are ground ivy and elder.

- Before the group arrive, mark out 3 'wolf territories', with 1 oil for each territory, by dropping some oil on to a large stone, fallen tree or tree trunk, as a scent marker.

- Do not overlap wolf territories but keep them in view of each other. The older or more experienced the players, the larger each territory can be.

- Explain that wolves mark their territories by urinating in key places. No two wolves leave the same smell, so boundaries are easily distinguished.

- Divide the group into 3 wolf packs. Each pack is assigned one of the scents.

- Choose an 'alpha wolf' and scent his or her ankle to match the territory.

- The game begins with the other wolves in each pack sniffing the scent on their alpha wolf and then trying to find the edges of their territory.

- Once all wolves have found their perimeter, they howl. The game ends when the alpha wolf stands in the centre of the territory and is joined by his or her pack.

Grey wolf (*Canis lupus*)

Invisible learning

This activity provides a good starting point for discussing the social structure in a wolf pack, which is based on a dominant male and female. Consider the body language used by other, subservient, animals. It is a great way to appreciate the importance of smell, boundaries and working in a team.

Deer stalk

Apache children played this game as a way to learn to hunt and get close enough to touch a deer's tail!

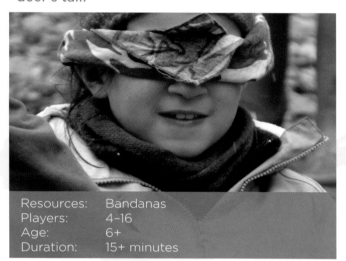

Resources:	Bandanas
Players:	4–16
Age:	6+
Duration:	15+ minutes

How to

- Ask for a volunteer deer. This person is blindfolded and an adult is the adjudicator.
- Gather the group into a circle and ask the deer to sit in the middle. The group then walks 10 paces out from the deer.
- Put a bandana into the deer's pocket or the back of the trousers so that it can be easily seen.
- When everything is ready, the group starts to quietly and slowly make its way towards the deer, attempting to take the bandana from the deer without being heard.
- If the deer hears someone approaching they must point directly at them, at which point that person is out.
- The deer has 3 chances of wrongly pointing towards someone.

- **Warning:** The group should not throw sticks or stones as a way of making a noise. The adult needs to be clear whether someone is out or not, and can ask the group to freeze while checking the angle of the pointed finger!
- The game ends when either someone gets the bandana or all the stalkers are out.

Variations

- Place as many bandanas as people around the deer. The mission is to take a bandana without being pointed at and get back to where you started.
- Make a pile of leaves by the deer and put sticks in the leaves (like a woodland hedgehog). Stalk in quietly and remove a stick and get back without being heard or pointed at.

Invisible learning

This is an ideal way to slow down, relax and expand your senses and awareness. The aim is not to be the first, but to be the most skilful hunter – to stalk the prey and get close enough without being heard. As the deer, your hearing is acutely engaged and you draw on natural intuition and instinct to locate other players.

Wildcats prowling

This game is a nature-based version of grandmother's footsteps.

Resources:	None
Players:	4–30
Age:	4+
Duration:	10+ minutes

How to

- Set the scene by asking if anyone has seen a cat stalking a bird or a mouse.
- An adult starts as a rabbit or other prey animal and pretends to graze while facing away from the group.
- The rest of the players are hungry wildcats. They begin the game on an imaginary line some distance (at least 10m) away from the rabbit.
- When everyone is in position, the wildcats stalk their prey on all fours.
- When the rabbit hears something or is alerted to danger, he or she turns round. If anyone is moving, they are named and sent back to the starting line to rejoin the game.
- The winner is the wildcat who successfully reaches the rabbit without alerting him or her, making them the best hunter.

Variations

- Try this game in different natural settings such as in meadows with long grass or woodland clearings.
- Play the game as lions prowling and hunting deer.

Fact

Deer see only in black and white and are highly attuned to observe danger through movement.

Most prey animals have limited vision and see movement better than form. If a cat is perfectly still when a bird looks towards it, it often goes unnoticed.

Wildcat (*Felis silvestris*)

Invisible learning

This activity encourages stealth movement and sensory awareness for both the predator and the prey. Taking the role of an animal gives players freedom to move in a different way and embody the movements of that animal. Playing in a variety of environments allows players to learn how to move quietly in a range of terrains and to understand what kinds of movement are most effective in diverse contexts.

Awareness trail

What are your blind spots; what goes unseen all around you? Who is watching you?

Resources:	objects
Players:	1–16
Age:	4+
Duration:	20+ minutes

How to

- Decide on a stretch of natural space that has interesting plants and trees on both sides, and a path that can be walked.
- On either side of the path, set up a trail using a variety of man-made and natural objects, e.g. bandana, fork, skull, shell, hat, feather – whatever you have!
- Ask the players to walk along the path, making a mental note of how many objects they see.
- When they reach the end, ask how many they have seen (without naming them) and then ask them to walk back, repeating the exercise.

- What makes the objects stand out? Is it the texture or colours? Were some more camouflaged than others?
- On the third and final walk, ask the group to count on their fingers how many objects they see.

Hat?

Paintbrush?

Feather and shell?

Invisible learning

At the heart of this game is the development of awareness: awareness of yourself, of others and of your surroundings – they are life skills.

This activity raises lots of questions about how animals hide and survive.

String walk

What would a journey through a wild landscape feel like without your eyes?

Resources: Bandanas, rope
Players: 2–16
Age: 4+
Duration: 15+ minutes

How to

- Tie a long rope around objects along a route at least 30 paces long, with some variation in terrain.
- Bring the group to the start point already blindfolded (see Blindfolded caterpillar, p.77).
- One by one, lead them to the start of the rope and tell them to follow the rope as their guide. Invite them to take their time and ask them not to let go of the rope, encouraging them to walk in silence.
- Have someone meet them at the other end of the rope.
- When everyone has completed the route, ask a few questions about the experience, then ask the players to walk the route with their eyes open. How was it different?

Variations

- If the group is up for it, invite them to try the walk barefoot!
- You can set up an awareness trail (see p.66) alongside the string walk to do next. After doing the trail blindfolded and sighted, tell the group there are several objects of interest out there, and ask them to follow the route again sighted and see what they notice.
- Complete the walk using fox walking (see p.57), as this way of moving will keep you safe.

Invisible learning

This activity can be a challenge for some and many will feel a real sense of achievement once they complete the blindfolded walk. It allows people to have an individual experience and develop trust in their other senses. By the end of the walk, most people seem to relax, moving with care and in a calm state.

Jedi training

Balancing on a tree beam

Resources:	Fallen tree trunks
Players:	1–30
Age:	3+
Duration:	15+ minutes

How to

- Find or create an area with fallen tree limbs that are challenging to balance on from one end to the other. **NOTE: Assess the tree trunks carefully to ensure that they are not rotten, are stable and are an appropriate height for the age of the group.**

- Ensure the surroundings are not hazardous, e.g. tree stumps or protruding branches.

- Ask each player to walk along the trunk(s). A progression of challenges could include:
  - Walk the beam without support.
  - Walk the beam looking straight ahead using owl eyes (see p.58).
  - Walk the beam backwards.
  - Move along the beam on all fours.
  - Walk the beam holding a glass of water, trying not to spill it.
  - Walk the beam blindfolded.

- It can be great fun to have face-offs, where two people are on a beam, each holding a fern or long feather (e.g. a pheasant tail feather), and they can use these to try and distract and tickle the other off the beam. Last player standing wins!

Invisible learning

This helps to develop balance and motor skills, but perhaps more pronounced is the confidence building that comes from the sense of achievement. It is great to develop children's sense of proprioception.

Head honcho

Many moving as one.

Resources: None
Players: 6+
Age: 7+
Duration: 10+ minutes

How to

- Form everyone in a circle, standing about an arm's distance apart.
- Ask one person to be the detective and leave the group (somewhere out of sight and earshot).
- Have the group silently pick a head honcho.
- The head honcho instigates a movement, e.g. stamping feet, clicking fingers, rubbing tummy, and all the others in the circle copy him or her.
- The head honcho must continually change the movement.
- The detective is invited back to the group and from one spot in the middle of the circle must try and guess who is changing the movement. He or she has 3 attempts.
- The others must try not to give away the head honcho, while keeping up with the changes in movement.

Variations

- Have 2 detectives.
- Restrict movements to waist up.

Invisible learning

A great ice-breaker to ease people into working together, head honcho is a very creative game that can produce some novel movements.

The detectives have a good opportunity to expand their senses and their observation skills. Those within the group also have to practise their peripheral vision to prevent giving away the head honcho.

Treasure hunt

A mapping game.

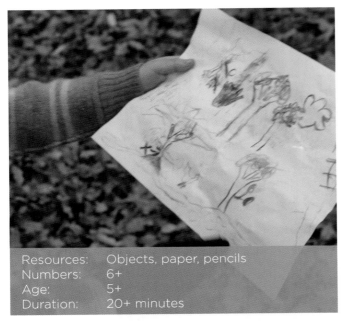

Resources: Objects, paper, pencils
Numbers: 6+
Age: 5+
Duration: 20+ minutes

How to

- Split your group into teams of about 3.
- Give each team an object that stands out in your environment, such as an orange.
- Tell each team to hide their object, within set boundaries, for another team to find. Once they have hidden it, they need to draw a map showing where it is hidden.
- Give them an appropriate time frame – 5 to 15 minutes – to achieve this.
- Once the teams have hidden their objects and drawn their maps, each team must swap maps with another team and go on a treasure hunt to find the hidden objects.

Variations

- Create 3D maps using sticks, moss or earth to represent the landscape.
- With older children and adults, this activity can be extended to teach orienteering by writing bearings or instructions to find the object.

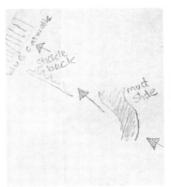

Invisible learning

This is a really fun introduction to mapping and navigation, as it brings attention to landmarks. What in the natural world can be used as a signpost?

Pyramid game

Have fun learning about food chains.

Resources:	Home-made trophic level cards, food pyramid diagram
Numbers:	10+
Age:	10+
Duration:	15+ minutes

A trophic level is the feeding position that an organism occupies in a food chain. For example, primary producers, including green plants, form trophic level 1, herbivores form trophic level 2, primary carnivores form trophic level 3, etc.

There must be more individuals at lower tropic levels.

For more information and examples see www.greenbooks.co.uk/lwn-resources

How to

- Make one trophic level card for each player in a team. The number of cards on each level must match the pyramid players will build.

- Show players a diagram of a food chain depicting the various trophic levels. Divide the group into teams.
- The object of the game is to see which team can build its pyramid and label each level first.
- Try 4 players on the bottom, 2 on the next row and 1 at the top!
- Only correct labelling counts – the cards can be hung from their necks or held in their mouths.

Variations

- Use flora and fauna from different ecosystems, e.g. the sea, woods, rainforest, desert, mountains.
- If you do not want to create a human pyramid, especially for larger food chains, arrange the cards on the ground instead.

Invisible learning

This fun activity teaches young people about food chains in a practical way. It builds cooperative skills and opens the discussion about the ecosystem.

What would happen if one part of the food chain was eliminated, due to overfishing or an oil spill, for example?

75

Electric pulse

What is the group's heart rate?

Resources: None
Players: 8+
Age: 6+
Duration: 5+ minutes

How to

- Ask your group to form a circle, with one person leading the game.
- Ask everybody to place their RIGHT thumb in the LEFT palm of the person to their RIGHT (see photos). The circle should be connected!
- The leader makes a noise or says a word at the same time as pressing his or her thumb on the palm of the person to the right.
- When each person feels the 'pulse', they pass it on, completing the circuit. It should eventually arrive back at the person who initiated the first pulse.

Variations

- Ask people to close their eyes.
- The first round is usually the slowest – we often liken this to the heartbeat of a cow. Aim to raise the heartbeat to that of a deer, then to a shrew's!

Shrew (*Sorex araneus*)

Invisible learning

By inviting the participants to work together using their sense of touch, the game shows that with focus and a deeper listening, we can move in unison at great speed! It is also a good way to gauge how awake the group is!

Blindfolded caterpillar

In many cultures people used to journey in a line, one behind the other. They appeared as one body with many legs, like a caterpillar!

Resources: Bandanas, rope
Players: 4–15
Age: 4+
Duration: 10+ minutes

How to

- Ask the group to get into a line.
- Give each participant a blindfold.
- A length of rope is held by one sighted leader at the front and another at the back of the line. Ask each person to hold onto the rope using their left hand so that the rope is on one side of the line. It is a good idea to also have one or two adults at each side to keep the group safe.
- Agree some basic aids, e.g. if someone needs to stop, say 'stop', and the group will halt. Encourage the group to listen for all sounds and notice the different smells and textures of the land beneath their feet.

Variations

- Get a member of the group to have a turn at leading the caterpillar, and continue to rotate the leader.
- Walk as a caterpillar by gently holding on to the shoulder of the person in front instead of a rope.

Invisible learning

Being blindfolded can be a challenging step and involves a degree of trust. Taking a risk brings a sense of achievement and facilitates a change in perception towards the natural surroundings.

When the dominant sense (eyesight) is lost, the other senses compensate and you are able to hear much more, and have a heightened sense of balance, texture, light and dark. Walking in silence with a group can be a profound experience.

There is nothing simpler than wandering the land with child-like exploration. Given the space, the right environment and the freedom, this is exactly what children do naturally. They discover worlds in roots of trees, jungles when crawling through waist-high grasses, small creatures hidden in cities on the banks of streams. Once we let go of sticking to the paths or our own agendas of getting from A to B, there are worlds to be encountered, marvelled at and played in, even in the most unlikely places.

As a family out on a walk, allow time for free play and let the children lead you on an adventure. As parents, we need to strike a balance between letting ourselves enter the imaginative worlds that children inhabit and keeping the family safe. In order to do this, a map and compass is necessary in unfamiliar and large natural spaces. You could also carry a mobile phone and check it has reception in case of difficulty. Alternatively, rich wandering experiences can happen even in your local park by bringing this attitude of play and exploration to your walk.

Aimless wandering is timeless, enabling us to be guided by nature itself and by our instincts. When we are in the moment, we are most likely to experience the magical wonders that are going on around us all the time. These are the times we come across a frog and catch it, when we get to watch a spider spinning its web, or stumble upon a sleeping fawn.

Tool safety pp.82-83   Wild facts pp.84-85

Birds

- Nests and eggs
- Pine-cone feeders
- Birds on a stick
- Sit spot

Animals

- Bug hotel
- Tracking
- Trailing
- Natural camouflage

Plants

- Natural fibre cordage
- Leaf prints
- Leaf tiles
- Flower fairies

Trees

- Elder pencils
- Woodland jewellery
- Woodcraft
- Raft making

All equipment needs to be kept in a safe place when not in use and needs regular and effective maintenance. Do not wear gloves on the hand that is holding the tool, as this compromises your grip and reduces your tool control.

When using a tool for the first time, take a moment to become aware of sharp edges and how this particular tool works.

Always have a first aid kit with you and make sure someone knows how to administer it. Always put tools away in their sheaths when not in use and never leave tools unattended.

Knives

Knives are incredibly useful. To help prevent unnecessary cuts or wounds, here are some considerations.

- Keep your knives sharp – a sharp knife is much safer than a blunt one.
- With groups of young people in your care, knives should be kept in a locked box.
- Use knives in good light conditions and when everyone is alert.
- Do not walk or stand with a knife when whittling.
- Make sure nobody is within arm's length of you when using a knife.
- For general whittling, sit down, place your elbows on your knees and always whittle away from yourself. This protects your body, especially your upper legs where there are major arteries.
- Appropriate adult supervision is required.

Away from the body

Palm drill

Palm drills

- Find a safe working space and flat surface.
- Keep your hands out of danger – the sides of the drill bit are sharp as well as the point.
- Check the bit is set before use.

Saws

Always find a suitable work surface to use. When sawing, be mindful of your clothing and keep sleeves out of the way.

Bowsaw

- Replace the safety cover over the blade when not in use.
- Carry the saw at arm's length, parallel to the ground.
- Put the non-sawing hand through the saw to steady the wood being sawn. This protects the non-sawing hand.

Pruning saw

- When using a folding pruning saw, keep your hands away from the teeth when folding it.
- Put your non-sawing hand over the saw when sawing.

Birds

- Robins are one of the few birds to sing through the winter, and, unusually, both males and females sing.

- A baby blue tit's parents are very busy, as the babies can eat around 1,000 insects a day.

- Jays have great memories and can remember where they have hidden hundreds of acorns. Naturally, they forget some and so help oak trees to spread.

- Kestrels can see ultraviolet light, which enables them to detect the urine trails of the rodents they are hunting.

Animals

- The pygmy shrew needs to eat its own bodyweight in food every 24 hours to survive.

- A badger sett (den) can be passed down through the generations for hundreds of years.

- Rabbits recycle their pooh! They eat soft droppings in their burrows to get more nutrients from them; the droppings we usually see are the second batch, which they don't eat.

- A pipistrelle bat can eat 3,000 midges in one night.

European robin
(*Erithacus rubecula*)

Daisies
(*Bellis perennis*)

Badger (*Meles meles*)

English oak tree
(*Quercus robur*)

Plants

- Daisies close up at night and during dull weather. This is how they got their original name, 'day's eye'.

- Four different kinds of British butterfly need nettles to provide food for their caterpillars.

- A bramble shoot can grow 7.5cm in a day. The fresh leaves, also known as bramble tips, are edible in the spring.

- Seaweed contains a gloopy substance that is used in toothpaste and even ice cream.

Trees

- Yew is the oldest living British tree. The Fortingall Yew in Perthshire is thought to be c.5000 years old – as old as Stonehenge.

- Large beech trees can drop branches without warning, so it is best to avoid camping beneath them!

- Oak trees support more wildlife than any other British tree.

- A large tree can take up more than 500 litres of water a day.

Nests and eggs

Handmade nest with clay eggs

Bird nests are quite incredible. There are so many different types made from different materials, each cleverly designed and constructed with simply two feet and a beak. Long-tailed tits make intricate homes using lichens and spider webs to create elastic nests that expand as the chicks grow! They collect over 1,000 feathers to line each nest and fly between 600 and 700 miles to collect the materials.

How to

- To introduce this activity, spend time in the spring watching the birds and looking for nests in the local environment.
- It is helpful to bring pre-gathered nest-building materials. The best materials often happen to be those that are good for tinder bundles (see fire lighting, p.178), such as dried sticky grass, dry grass or dry bracken.
- To make a nest, take a rough bundle of grass, make a loop and then weave in the ends to create a nest-like shape.
- Give the nests to the children, who can forage in the forest for soft linings to complete them, such as bits of moss, lichen and feathers. Be careful not to take too much!
- Consider how many eggs different birds may lay in one clutch and make clay eggs. Many eggs are speckled, and when the clay egg is gently rolled on the forest floor, the speckled effect is very realistic.

Resources

- Clay
- Nesting material
- Naturalist books (optional)

Variations

- Combine this activity with an Easter egg hunt, using the nests to gather chocolate eggs.
- Discover which birds live in your garden or local woodland. Which of them are ground, mid-canopy or top-canopy dwellers? Do they live in nests all year round or only when breeding?
- Paint the eggs.
- Take undyed sheep's wool and leave strands on branches for woodland birds to use in their nests. It is exciting to come back later and find they have disappeared!

Top tips

- Many environments have suitable resources but, just in case, take a large bag of nest-building materials.
- Carry out this activity during the height of the nesting season.
- Avoid going close to nests during nesting season, as the parent birds will abandon a disturbed nest. Use binoculars instead.

Invisible learning

- Seasonal awareness.
- Empathy and relationship building.
- Increases bird knowledge.
- Use of natural materials.

Related activities

Nest robbers p.45   Sit spot pp.92-93
Evergreen wreath and crown pp.152-53

Pine-cone feeders

How to

- Gather pine cones, enough for at least 1 each.
- Mix together fat and birdseed in a bowl. Children can do this with their hands.
- At the pointed top of the pine cone, tightly tie a string for hanging.

- Ask the children to squash the fat and seed mix into and around the pine cone. The result will look like a fat ball.
- Tie the cones to a tree as a gift to the birds.

This is a particularly good activity during the winter months, when times are hard for the birds, but it can be fun to do at any time of year.

Resources

- Fat (lard, nut butter, solid vegetable fat)
- Bird seed
- Pine cones
- String

Variations

- Tell a story about birds before making the feeders.
- Do some birdwatching and discover where the birds hang out ... This might be a good place to hang your feeder.
- Create a naturalist profile on a specific type of bird. Find out all about it: what it eats, where it lives, when it has young.
- Use palm drills to make holes in a piece of wood and fill these with your bird food mixture.

Coal tit (*Periparus ater*)

Top tips

- This is a messy activity so it is best done outside where the birds can clear up for you.
- Mix wild edible berries into your bird food mixture.
- Have warm soapy water to wash your hands in afterwards.

Invisible learning

- Caretaking the natural world.
- Identification of seeds.
- Awareness of birds and their habits.
- Empathy.

Related activities

Nest robbers p.45   Bug hotel pp.94-95
Swallow migration pp.126-27

Messy...but fun!

Birds on a stick

Have you ever looked closely at our native birds? Each species has distinctive and beautiful feather patterns and colours.

How to

- Gather long, thin, very dry sticks.
- Using a field guide, choose a common songbird, e.g. a chaffinch or blackbird, and copy the shape of wings and body onto a folded piece of thin card (photo A).
- Cut out templates for the wings and two of the body (photos B).
- Colour the wings and body as shown in your field guide; notice the symmetry of the patterns (see photo C).
- Stick the body parts together and fold down top flaps (photo D).
- Put double-sided sticky tape on the two flaps and on the central fold of the wings (photo E).
- Join the bird parts to the stick (photos D and E).
- Form a crease on the wings by folding up and down several times, this helps the wings to flap freely when flown.

A

B

Resources

- A4 card
- Scissors
- Oil pastels or coloured pencils
- Double-sided sticky tape
- Bird field guide book
- Long, thin sticks

Variations

- For younger children, cut out the birds first and let them colour freely. Stick parts together for them.
- Let older children choose any bird and make their own design templates of the wing and body shapes.
- Choose a bird that regularly visits the bird table or your sit spot. Learn the song and habit of your chosen bird.
- Make a mobile with your birds.

Top tips

- Use pastels for colouring.
- To make blackbirds, use black card.
- Practise making templates before doing the activity with a group.

Invisible learning

- Close observation of any species helps deepen understanding and appreciation.
- Increases natural pattern recognition.

Related activities

Swallow migration pp.126-27   Painted beetles pp.128

Sit spot

How to

- Start this activity with a sense meditation (see p.60).

- Invite each person to find their own special place in the surrounding area, giving clear, appropriate boundaries, and near enough to hear the call to come back.

- Before they go, give the children a goal to listen to as many sounds as they can. How many birds can they hear or see? Point out that the quieter they are on the way to their spot, the less disturbed the birds will be. Encourage fox walking (see p.57).

- Send them out. Depending on the group, they could stay out for 5 to 20 minutes for a first sit spot.

- When they come back, ask them what noises they heard, whether they saw any wildlife, whether they noticed anything unusual. Find out how it felt for them to be sitting in their own special space in nature.

Wherever you are in the world, birds and other animals are in constant communication. To the untrained ear this has no meaning, but with time and patience you can start to recognise patterns that report what is happening in the world around you.

Listen out for these 5 voices of the birds. They are the basics to understanding the language of birds as documented by Jon Young in audio recordings and his book *What the Robin Knows*.

- **Song** Birds do simply sing for the joy of it. Birdsong is heard most often at the dawn chorus.
- **Companion calls** These are often heard when birds are feeding together, especially between a male and female that have partnered up for the season. It is their way of making sure that they know where the other is and that everything is OK.
- **Territorial aggression** In spring, finding a mate and holding their territory is important. When you hear sharp, angry-sounding tones made by just one species of bird, it is likely to be sorting out a territorial issue.
- **Juvenile begging** This is the squawking you hear in spring from a nest full of chicks begging for their food.
- **Alarm calls** These signal a threat. Ground predators, e.g. a fox, are often cheeped at angrily by songbirds, who are high enough to be out of reach. This cheeping may follow the predator around, indicating where it is. Aerial predators, e.g. sparrowhawks, create a sudden danger, so birds must stay still and quiet to avoid being eaten. In this way, tunnels of silence are created in the fabric of bird sound in the woods.

Variations

- After the sit spot, draw a map of the area and ask individuals to mark sounds that they heard on the map. Discover whether several people were aware of the same bird or series of bird calls.
- Go back to the same sit spot time after time and experience how it changes through the seasons.
- Bring attention to different aspects of the sit spots. How many different plants grow there? What signs of animal activity are there? Where do the insects like to hang out?

Wren (*Troglodytes troglodytes*)

Top tips

- Ask the group to sit far enough away from each other.
- Share stories from your sit spot to inspire others.

Invisible learning

- Cultivating a quiet mind.
- Feeling at home in nature.
- Heightened awareness.

Related activities

Fox walking p.57   Owl eyes p.58
Deer ears p.59   Sense meditation p.60

Bug hotel

Insects love small spaces and you can make bug hotels to help them out. Bug hotels of many shapes and sizes all provide the perfect habitat for insects such as ladybirds, lacewings, spiders and even lone bees.

How to

- Get inspired by minibeasts: look at some pictures of them and then go on an insect hunt with a magnifying glass. Moving big logs is often a good place to find them.

- To create a small box about the size of a bird box, use a plank of wood. Saw sections: 15 x 15cm for the base, 15 x 20cm for the sides and two 15 x 15cm sections for the roof. Nail them together.

- Choose a plant, such as elder or buddleia, that grows in such a way as to allow you to make hollow tubes from its stems. Use loppers to cut it into lengths to fit your box.

- Use a metal tent peg to push the pithy centre out of the stems leaving hollow tubes.

- You could also drill different-sized holes into a log to make diverse rooms for the insects.

- Arrange all the stems in the box and pack them tightly.

- Find a spot in the garden or local woods to leave your bug hotel and stop by in a few weeks to see if it has any visitors!

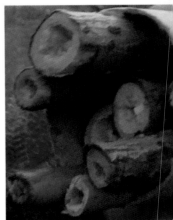

Resources

- Buddleia or elder
- Loppers
- Metal tent peg
- Palm drill
- Plank of wood
- Nails
- Hammer

Variations

- Create wooden model bugs by drilling holes and using sticks for legs.
- Cultivate curiosity about insects by asking questions such as what do they eat? And what do they have to watch out for in case they get eaten?

Invisible learning

- Introduction to conservation.
- Principles of caretaking.
- Wood properties.
- Understanding habitats.
- Knowledge of invertebrates.

If you want to take it to another level, here is what one family created with bits and pieces they had lying around.

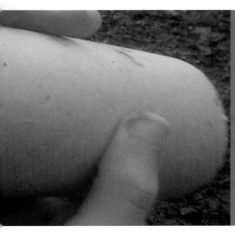

A simple version of this activity is to use the elder and buddleia, but instead of putting them in a box, bind them with string or put them inside a toilet roll.

Top tip

- If you are struggling to push the pith out of the stems, try shorter sections and make sure you don't have branch junctions within the section.

Related activities

Wildlife is watching p.55   Painted beetles pp.128-29
Teasel hedgehogs pp.142-43

Tracking

Fox track

Everyone loves animals, but it is not often that we get to see them. However, they are always leaving tracks and signs behind for us to find.

How to

- Have a brainstorming session about what evidence animals might leave behind.
- Look at some pictures of different tracks and signs.
- Go out in search of tracks of all kinds:
  - Animal footprints
  - Hair and fur
  - Feeding signs: nibbled nuts, pine cones, browsed shoots
  - Frequently used trails
  - Homes: holes in the ground, trees, nests
  - Day beds – compressed areas of terrain.

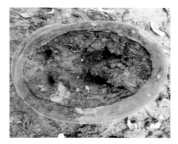

Deer track

Track casts

If you find a good footprint of an animal track, take a plaster cast of it to preserve the shape of the footprint like a fossil.

- Choose the track you are going to cast.
- Create a perimeter around the track by pushing a strip of plastic or thin card into the ground to surround the track (old bottles or cereal boxes work well).
- Make the mix: approximately 1 cup of water per cast. Then sprinkle the plaster of Paris into the water until it builds up to reach the surface. Use a clean stick to mix the plaster and water into a consistency like custard.
- Pour the mix into the track and leave to set (at least 30 minutes).
- Go back to your track and remove the dry plaster cast. When it comes out of the ground, it will have some bits attached. Just like an archaeologist, you can carefully remove the debris from your cast.

WARNING: do not dip your fingers in setting plaster – it becomes hot as it sets.

Resources

- Plastic or card strips to surround the track
- Plaster of Paris
- Cups
- Water
- Clean stick

Variations

- Start the session by telling an inspiring tracking story.
- Learn more about the animals you are tracking by making an animal profile. Find out what it eats, where it sleeps, what eats it, what its habits are, what time of day or night it is active. All this will help you find its tracks and trails.

Invisible learning

- Builds connection with animals.
- Develops skills of shapes and pattern recognition.
- Stimulates curiosity about animals.

Top tip

- Clay and sand are great for tracks. If you know where an animal trail is but the earth is too hard, you can leave sand on it as a track trap and check for tracks the next day.

Related activities

Master tracker p.53   Trailing pp.98-99
Natural camouflage pp.100-01

Badger track

Stoat (*Mustela erminea*)

Trailing

It is hard to match the excitement and anticipation of being hot on a trail, not knowing where it will lead you next...

How to

- Split the group into two teams; one starts as the trail makers, the other as the trackers.
- The trackers occupy themselves for 5 minutes to give the trail makers time to set the trail.
- The trail makers take a big stick and set off in a line, treading in each other's footsteps and dragging the stick behind them to leave a clear but at times challenging trail in addition to their footprints.
- After they have gone a fair distance, the trail makers can leave the stick, and camouflage themselves in the undergrowth along or near the end of the trail. Now they wait, quiet as mice!
- The trackers begin tracking from the agreed start point and pick up the trail. They look for signs of disturbance in the ground and follow the trail through the landscape.
- When they get to the end of the trail, they must keep their wits about them and look out for where the others are camouflaged.
- Once the trail makers have all been found, ask the teams to swap roles.

Resources

- Camouflage materials (optional)
- Big stick

Variations

- To make this activity more challenging, lift the stick up for a few paces from time to time.

Invisible learning

- Develops skills of detecting disturbances in the terrain.
- Encourages teamwork.
- Introduces a need to be quiet and stealthy.

Top tips

- Think of a 5 to 10 minute activity for one team while the other team sets up the trail. The 'deer ears' game is a good one (see p.59)!
- The trick is to make the trail challenging enough but visible enough for the trackers to succeed in finding the end of the trail.

Related activities

Wildlife is watching p.55
Tracking pp.96-97 . Natural camouflage pp.100-01

Natural camouflage

Natural camouflage is how to become invisible in the forest. It is fun and instinctive, and provides the essence of adventure!

How to

- Set the scene by asking the group how often they see an animal in the wild. Why don't we see animals more often?
- Why are they hard to see? Camouflage. Explain the different kinds of camouflage – colours similar to the forest, or patterns and shapes that disguise the animal's shape.
- Some natural camouflage colours include: black using crushed charcoal from a previous fire or cooled from the current fire; brown, mixing water with clay; and white, crushing chalk to make a white powder.
- Paint each other's faces.
- Use your camouflage to play some games, such as wolves and deer (see p.54), wildlife is watching (see p.55) and eagle eye (see p.47).
- It is nice to be able to wash the camouflage off in a bowl of warm water at the end.

Resources

- Charcoal
- Clay
- Chalk
- Water
- Large plastic washing-up bowl for water
- Kettle for warming water over a fire

Spot the camouflaged person!

Invisible learning

- Body sense of being a predator or prey – an experiential, primitive response.
- Getting beyond 'yuck, it's dirty!'
- Camouflage and concealment – how it is used in the army, to watch wildlife and even by ancient Apache scouts to evade the enemy!
- Cultivating a quiet mind when being still and blending in.

Top tip

- Avoid wood ash as it makes an alkaline that in high concentration in liquid can burn your skin. Avoid using baby wipes due to the waste they produce – warm water and a dry towel work better.

Related activities

Eagle eye p.47 Wolves and deer p.54
Wildlife is watching p.55 Sit spot pp.92-93

101

Natural fibre cordage

How to

- A basic way to make cordage (string) from natural plant fibres is to use raffia, which can be bought online and in garden shops.
- Ask the group to work in pairs: each holds one end of the raffia and faces each other.
- The partners must stand so that the raffia is taut, and both twist to their right or their left. Ask them to keep twisting until the raffia holds a lot of tension and starts kinking. Hold it tight and do not let go.

- While holding the raffia, and not letting it twist up on itself, a third person must pinch the middle while the pair comes together to fold the raffia in half.
- When the person holding the middle lets go, the raffia will wrap itself into string.

RAFFIA

STINGING NETTLE

BRAMBLE

Cordage is one of the oldest and most useful technologies. Its uses can extend from practical survival situations to creating beautiful jewellery and art. It is also a great way to discover the resources hidden within the natural world.

A more precise and advanced technique follows (described for right-handed people):

- With this cordage method, participants work on their own with the natural plant fibres.
- Find the middle point (the fold) of your fibres and make one end a few centimetres longer than the other.
- Pinch the fold between your left thumb and index finger.
- Take one of the strands, about 3cm from the fold, and begin to twist it away from you until the fibres feel tight.
- Swap the strands over by twisting them both towards you.
- Continue until one strand is almost finished (about 3cm remaining).
- To lengthen your cordage, splice in another piece of raffia by overlaying it and twisting it into the shortest end.

Resources

- Raffia or other plant fibres e.g. nettle or bramble

Completed cordages

Top tip

- Ensure that you have the hang of this before teaching it to a group. The activity can take perseverance and is most easily taught by demonstration.

Invisible learning

- Patience.
- Focus and concentration.
- Ancient skills.
- Raw materials.

Related activities

Plants and trees games pp.34–41
Woodland jewellery pp.112-13

Leaf prints

This inspiring activity helps bring to life the patterns and plants in our environment in a creative way.

How to

- Cut some calico or a white cotton sheet to the desired size.
- Find a hard, flat surface that it is safe to dent – a tree stump works well.
- Gather some fresh leaves and flowers (only use common, abundant plants). Arrange in a pattern on one half of the cloth.

WARNING: avoid poisonous species

- Fold the blank half over to sandwich the leaves and flowers inside.
- Use a hammer to repeatedly hit the cloth all over. As you do so, a beautiful pattern will emerge.
- Open out the cloth and remove excess plant material.
- As a group, share and admire each other's leaf prints.

Resources

- Calico or cotton
- Scissors
- Hard, flat surface (e.g. chopping boards or tree stumps)
- Hammers, mallets or rounded sticks
- Common, abundant plants

Variations

- Create your own beautiful gathering bags with the leaf prints by sewing up the edges and adding a cordage handle (see p.102).
- Make a rustic picture frame from four sticks lashed together in the corners. You can sew the leaf prints on to the frame.
- This activity can help with plant identification and can be used in connection with foraging (see p.158).

Top tips

- This works best in spring and summer when leaves are fresh and full of moisture.
- It is helpful to demonstrate this activity first if doing it as a group.
- When cutting calico, you can simply snip the edge and then tear.

Invisible learning

- Leaf pattern recognition.
- Creativity and natural dyes.
- Hand-eye coordination.

Related activities

Plants and trees games pp.34–41

105

Leaf tiles

Each plant has unique and intricate patterns which we may not normally be aware of. This art activity provides a perfect way to draw attention to the beauty of these patterns.

How to

- Find a flat surface, such as a tree stump. Get a ball of clay and a rolling pin and roll the clay out. Use two sticks of the same diameter, about 1.5cm, as guides when rolling the clay, so that it is a uniform thickness (photo A).

- Choose a leaf or several leaves and arrange them on the flat surface of the clay.
- Lightly roll over them to embed them slightly in the clay (photo B).
- Carefully peel the leaves off and look at how the clay holds the details of the leaves. Can you see the veins or the marks of any hairs?
- Cut off the edges of the clay so you are left with a clay tile. Poke two holes at the top so that you can nail it to the wall or put a string through to hang it up, once it has been fired.
- If you want to fire your clay tiles, you need to leave them to dry for about a week.

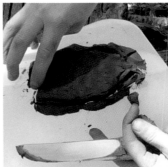

Resources

- Clay
- Rolling pin or smooth stick plus guide sticks
- Flat surface
- Baking paper (optional)
- Knife

Variations

- Create a simple pinch pot. Start with a ball of clay, push your thumbs into its middle and pinch around the edges until it is all about the same thickness. Once your pot is formed, push leaves into the outside to capture their impression.
- Create species-specific tiles e.g. oak leaf and acorn.
- Paint or glaze the tiles.

Top tips

- It is helpful to leave part of the leaf off the edge of the clay so you can easily peel it back.
- To prevent the clay sticking to the flat surface, put it on to a piece of baking paper.

Invisible learning

- Appreciation of the intricacy of plants.
- Reinforces plant identification.
- Uses the beauty of nature in art.

Related activities

Plants and trees games pp.34-41

107

Flower fairies

The UK is deeply imbued with fairy lore. When children go to the woods they love to play fairy games and look for their homes.

How to

- Write the names of nearby plants and trees on pieces of paper, fold them, and then put them in a hat. Ask the children to pick one each.
- The children must find their plant or tree, with help if needed.
- Give them a piece of clay and instructions to create a fairy using the parts of their plant.

Resources

- Clay
- Plant names on folded paper
- Hat

Variations

- Make a home for your fairy.
- Make a fairy picnic for all the fairies to come together. Gather wild foods, such as nuts and berries, and use leaves as plates, acorn cups as teacups, etc.
- Create stories or plays with the fairies.
- When the main activity focuses on one species of plant, e.g. elder when making cordial, everyone can make a fairy from this plant.
- Make non-specific plant fairies.

Top tips

- Only use common species and avoid any toxic or protected plants.
- Instruct children carefully on respectful gathering.
- Share the inspirational work of Cicely Mary Barker, whose illustrations and poetry about British plants and their fairies are brilliant resources. It can lead to children creating their own artwork and poetry about the plants.

Invisible learning

- Connecting to plants through creativity and imaginative play.
- Recognising plants.

Related activity

Fairy homes pp.168-69

109

Elder pencils

Elder (*Sambucus nigra*)

Transform wood into charcoal and create your own pencil.

How to

- Using secateurs, harvest some willow (0.5 to 1cm in diameter) and elder (1 to 1.5cm in diameter).
- Gather dry firewood and light a fire. (The fire will need to burn for 10-15 minutes.)
- Pierce two holes in the top of an old tin. Put the tin on the fire, to burn off any paper or glue. Take the tin off the fire and let it cool.
- Cut the willow into lengths to fit in your tin.
- Peel the willow, put it in the tin and put the lid on.
- Put the tin on the fire. The willow will be heated without oxygen, causing it to transform into charcoal rather than burn to ashes. After 2 minutes, smoke will stream out of the holes in the tin. Keep an eye on this: when the smoke stops take the tin off the fire.
- While the charcoal is cooking, use secateurs to cut a length of elder for the wooden part of the pencil.
- Use a metal tent peg to push in the pith about 2cm at one end of the piece of elder. This is where you will insert the piece of charcoal as the lead for your pencil.

- When the smoke has stopped streaming out of the holes in the tin lid, put your fire gloves on and carefully remove the tin from the fire. **DO NOT OPEN UNTIL COOL.**
- When the tin is cool, open up to find charcoal.
- Take a piece of charcoal that is about the same width as the hole in your elder and insert it, so that the charcoal lead extends 1 to 2cm out of the elder.
- Now test it out on a piece of paper or cloth.

Variations

- Decorate your pencil by using a whittling knife to make patterns in the bark or even take off the bark.
- Sharpen the elder stick to look more like a pencil before inserting the charcoal.

Resources

- Willow
- Elder
- Fire gloves
- Fire and plenty of wood
- Tin with replaceable lid
- Secateurs and/or loppers
- Peeler
- Metal tent pegs
- Paper or cloth

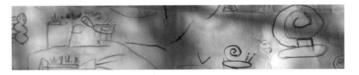

Invisible learning

- Teaches the effect of eliminating oxygen from the fire triangle (see fire lighting, p.178).
- Ancient skills, i.e. charcoal making.
- Uses of different trees.

Top tips

- Peel double the amount of willow you want, as they shrink during the process and some will break.
- A cloth easel works well, as paper can fly away or get soggy outdoors.
- If you take the tin off the fire and still find brown bits inside, put the lid back on and heat it again, making sure the fire under it is hot.

Related activities

Plants and trees games pp.34–41
Fire lighting pp.178–79

Woodland jewellery

Capture the natural beauty of wood by making a woodland medallion.

Medallion

- See tool safety, p.82, before starting.
- Find a branch of wood, with a diameter between 3 and 6cm, and harvest it in a respectful way.
- Each person needs a disc of wood approximately 1cm wide. These can be sawn by the young person where appropriate.
- Each person, in turn, uses a palm drill or brace and bit to make a hole near the perimeter of the disc – but not too close, as it may split.
- Thread a piece of string through the hole to make it into a necklace.

Resources

- String and tent peg
- Pruning saw or bowsaw, secateurs or loppers
- Palm drills 2–3mm in diameter or a brace and bit
- Sandpaper

Variations

- Write your name on the disc.
- Decorate the disc using paint or felt-tip pens. You could even draw or stamp animal tracks on them.
- Make natural cordage to replace the string.
- Vary the diameter and thickness of the discs to create a range of woodland bling, from rough-and-ready to fine pendants.
- Sand the disc (the wood must be seasoned, not green) and oil the medallion with a nut, e.g. a hazelnut or walnut (**check for nut allergies**).

Elder-bead necklace

As elder has a soft, pithy centre, it is very easy to make this wood into beads.

- Cut short lengths of elder – if green, use secateurs or loppers, if seasoned it is best to saw to avoid cracking.
- Use a metal tent peg or pencil to push out the pith.
- If you use seasoned elder, sand and oil the beads to shape.
- Make some natural cordage to thread the beads on.

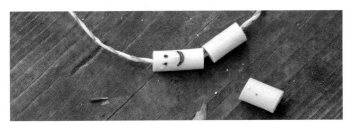

Invisible learning

- Develops fine motor skills.
- Promotes creativity.
- Teaches tool use and safe working methods.

Top tip

- If you use green wood, the medallions can crack as they dry, due to the loss of moisture, so use seasoned wood.

Related activities

Tool safety pp.82-83
Natural fibre cordage pp.102-3

Woodcraft

Mallet

- See tool safety, p.82, before starting.
- Harvest a piece of green wood about the size of an adult's forearm.
- Find the middle of the wood and use a saw to cut a little way into it, all the way around. The deeper you saw in, the thinner the handle will be. This is called a stop-cut.
- Decide which end is the handle and stand the mallet with the handle up.
- Place a knife on the handle end and use a solid stick to tap the knife down into the wood until you reach the stop-cut. At this point, that section of wood will fall away. Continue with this process all the way around the handle to thin it out.
- Whittle your handle so that it is more comfortable to hold.
- Your basic mallet is complete.

Woodcraft is addictive! Here are some things you can make while out adventuring.

Resources

- Green wood
- Saw
- Knife
- Loppers
- Solid stick
- Tree stump for carving on

Butter knife

- Use loppers or a saw to harvest some straight, green, non-toxic wood, approximately 2cm in diameter and 15cm long. Hazel or sweet chestnut works well.
- Find the middle of the stick.
- Decide which end will be the handle and which the blade.
- With your knife, carve the blade end, taking care to create two flat, parallel sides (avoid forming a point).
- Decorate the handle, for example by carving patterns into the bark.

Top tips

- First, show the children how to use the tools safely.
- When carving designs into the handle of the butter knife, it is helpful to have a tree stump to lean on.

Invisible learning

- Safe tool use.
- Fine motor skills.
- Uses of different woods.
- Coppicing and pruning awareness.

Related activities

Looking after nature pp.18-21
Tool safety pp.82-83

Raft making

There are many ways to make rafts, but this is a good starting point.

How to

This is a basic raft and is great fun to float down little streams.

- Find 4 to 8 sticks that are fairly straight, about finger thick and as long as a pencil.
- Tie a piece of string around each end of the stick. Use a simple knot to leave two long ends.
- Adding one stick at a time, tie the sticks as closely as possible to each other.
- On the final stick, tie double knots to finish the raft.

Resources

- Sticks
- String

Variations

- Add simple sails made from leaves or fabric. Use clay to hold the mast on, or simply wedge the mast between the raft sticks if they are tied well enough.
- Whittle the sticks of the raft, carve patterns into the bark.
- Create clay creatures to ride on the raft.
- Make a catamaran by attaching the raft to 2 bigger sticks.
- Create a challenge to get a natural object across a stream or downstream without it getting wet.

Invisible learning

- Knots and weaving.
- Measuring and sorting.
- Properties of water.

Top tip

- Coppiced hazel often has long straight sticks that work well for rafts and similar projects.

Related activities

Looking after nature pp.18-21   Tool safety pp.82-83

Teas through the seasons pp.120-123

Spring

Pages 124-131

- Birch tapping
- Swallow migration
- Painted beetles
- Sticky-weed fun!

Summer

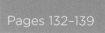

Pages 132-139

- Elderflower cordial
- Healing ointment
- Walnut boats
- Tree spirits

Autumn

Pages 140-147

- Waxed leaves
- Teasel hedgehogs
- Nut and berry flapjacks
- Clay gnomes

Winter

Pages 148-155

- Dutch oven bread
- Snow shelters
- Evergreen wreath and crown
- Pyrite wands

There are always wild plants in our local area that are available throughout the year to make tea. Drinking tea makes people feel more at home outdoors, as well as having direct interaction with the plants around them.

When working with groups of children, show them a leaf, then ask each child to find and bring back one or two of the same leaves. Introduce them to the plant's name and ask them questions about what they notice. Depending on their age, tell them about some of the healing properties of the plant. Then, make tea!

As a family or group going for a walk or day out, take flasks of boiled water and make teas from safe wild plants. This works well if you make the same tea a few times within a season, so that everyone becomes familiar with it.

Here is a selection of seasonal favourites that can usually be found in or at the edges of most British woodland (see foraging wild plants, p.158).

Spring

Nettle tea

Nettle (*Urtica dioica*)

Spring nettle tea has a wonderful, zingy freshness that children and adults alike enjoy. Either use gloves or be bold and pick off the tops: 'grasp the nettle'. Put plenty in the flask or pot, infuse and enjoy! Nettle has so many uses that there are books written about them (see further reading, pp.198-200).

Medicinal uses:

- High in vitamins and minerals.
- Externally used to bathe rashes, burns and stings.
- A natural antihistamine, helping hayfever.

Top tips

- Gather nettle tips in a bowl or basket and use scissors to cut them up.
- Only gather nettle leaves before the plant flowers, after which time it has a high concentration of uric acid.

Silver-birch tea

Silver birch (*Betula pendula*)

Birch is the tree of spring and new beginnings; it is sometimes called the oldest tree in Britain. It is the pioneer tree that grew here when the ice caps retreated, helping to make the soil fertile enough for other species. In the same way, it provides us with good medicine when the cold of winter retreats at last. Use the fresh green leaves plentifully in the pot.

Medicinal uses:

- An effective spring cleanse.
- Helps skin problems such as eczema.
- Relieves aching muscles.

Summer

Hawthorn-blossom tea

Hawthorn blossom (*Crataegus monogyna*)

Hawthorn flowers send their sweet scent on the breeze, filling the countryside on a warm summer day – this is known as the May wind. Hawthorn is the tree of the heart and protection; its thorny branches protect many birds and small mammals. Fill the pot with the blossoms when they are fresh and scented.

Medicinal uses:

- Heart tonic.
- Aids anxiety and insomnia.
- Crushed berries in the autumn can pull out splinters.

Linden-blossom tea

Lime / Linden blossom (*Tilia* species)

When the nectar-filled blossoms are ready, you may smell the tree before you see it, or hear the multitude of bees buzzing in its branches. The leaves are tasty in salads or in pesto, and the fresh blossoms make a delicious honey-tasting tea, wonderful for children.

Medicinal uses:

- Calming and soothing.
- Aids insomnia.
- Colds and fever.

Top tip

- The inner bark makes one of the best natural cordages (see pp.102-3), and the wood is ideal for fire by friction when seasoned.

Autumn

Rosehip tea

Rosehips (*Rosa canina*)

Nature provides us with just what we need. When autumn brings mists and cold nights, the change in the season often brings colds and flu. Thankfully, rosehips are one of the hedgerow berries that help us build strength and resilience. The hips are easy to identify and gather (watch out for the thorns, although they remind us of the protection this plant can give). Simmer the berries until soft enough to mash, then strain through a sieve lined with muslin or a clean cloth to remove the hairy seeds, which are irritants. It is well worth the effort!

Medicinal uses:

- A source of vitamin C.
- Soothes colds and sore throats.
- Relieves aching joints.

Blackberry (*Rubus fruticosus*)

This strong and determined plant is one of our most familiar and beneficial in its uses for making cordage, baskets, dyes, medicines and food.

Children have been eating blackberries in this land for thousands of years. As well as being a delectable wayside snack, the berries make very good tea when used in quantities, and can be added to other plant brews to make them tastier for children.

Medicinal uses:

- General health and a source of vitamin C.
- Helps sore throats and colds.

Top tips

- The young blackberry (bramble) leaves make a good tea in springtime.
- The fibres make excellent cordage.

Winter

Ground-ivy tea

Ground ivy (*Glechoma hederacea*)

This small creeping plant is a member of the mint family and is easily recognised by its strong aroma when rubbed between the fingers. It is one of the few plants that has leaves over winter, thus providing a health-giving tea during those cold frugal months. It flowers in March through to May.

Medicinal uses:

- Helps coughs and colds.
- Anti-inflammatory and antiseptic properties.
- Dries up congestion.
- Aids digestion.

Pine-needle tea

Scots pine (*Pinus sylvestris*)

This towering, stately tree is often a landmark in the forest and a favourite roosting place for birds such as buzzards and rooks. Its tall, straight trunk glows with an orangey-purple colour reminiscent of sunsets.

Throughout the year, its blue-green needles make a delicious tea full of vitamin C. This is particularly useful in the winter months, as it helps with coughs and colds both as a tea and as a steam inhalation.

Medicinal uses:

- Coughs and colds.
- Aids digestion.
- Its antiseptic and antibacterial properties are good for washing wounds.

Top tips

- If you simmer pine needles for a while, you may need to dilute the tea, as it can become very strong.
- Try adding a spoonful of honey.

Birch tapping

Silver birch (*Betula pendula*)

As your energy rises in springtime, so does the sap in the trees. People have always had a special relationship with silver birch: it symbolises new beginnings and we can drink its sap.

How to

- Select a strong and healthy silver birch tree that is at least 3 or 4 adult hand spans in circumference.
- The timing for tapping the birch is generally the first 2 weeks of March.
- To test that the sap is flowing, tap a knife into the bark a small way and watch for droplets of sap to appear.
- Drill a hole using a brace and bit (drill bit the same diameter as that of the tubing) 3 to 5cm into the tree.
- Insert plastic tubing into the hole, but not so far in that it touches the back of the hole. The sap needs some room to get into the tube.
- Put the other end of the tube into the mouth of a large container that is sitting at the base of the tree.
- Leave the sap to flow for 1 to 24 hours, depending on what is practical. The longer it can be left, the more sap will be gathered. If you can leave it until the following day, you should have a few litres of sap.

Resources

- Knife
- Brace and bit
- Drill bit, approx. 1.5cm in diameter to match tube
- Tubing, about 1m long and 1.5cm in diameter
- Large container
- Pruning saw

Top tips

- Instil a sense of gratitude by offering something to the tree.
- When the leaf buds begin to open on the hazel trees, it is the best time to tap the birch.
- It is helpful to seal the tube in the hole with soft beeswax or putty.
- Drink it while it's fresh. Although it can be preserved in a number of ways, birch sap is the essence of spring and has many medicinal properties that are most potent when drunk straight from the tree.

CAUTION: When you remove the tubing from the tree, it is very important to plug the hole with a freshly carved piece of wood that is tapered so it can be hammered tightly into the hole and any extra sawn off. If you do not do this, the tree will bleed out of the hole leaving an open wound that can lead to infection.

Invisible learning

- Tree identification.
- Cultivating respect for trees and their qualities.
- Relationship to the seasons.
- Understanding the responsibility of harvesting in a way that supports the natural world.
- Foraging knowledge.

Plug in birch tree

Related activities

Plants and trees games pp.34–41
Wild food pp.186–193

125

Swallow migration

As the sun warms, plants grow and insects emerge. Many birds return from far-off lands, including our much-loved swallow.

How to

- Make a swallow card cut-out, one for each person.
- Roll a lump of clay into a sausage shape. Cut the sausage of clay lengthways up to the head and slot the card template into the cut.
- Use a small twig to make holes for the eyes and then push the twig into the clay for the beak.
- Once your group has made the swallows, set the scene for their epic migration to Britain from Africa. Introduce their eating and sleeping habits and the kind of terrain they will be traversing.
- Hold the swallow on its underbelly between your thumb and forefinger, and off you go.
- The whole trip back – to the school, car park or house – is their journey. This is often an epic adventure for the children and many swallows don't make it back in one piece!

Resources

- Wings and tail made from cardboard
- Clay
- Compass for navigating the route (optional)

Variations

- Repeat this activity later in the year, when the swallows leave for Africa in August.
- Learn more about the swallow. Why not make a poster?
- Ask questions: how does the swallow know which way to go? Where will the sun be during the day? Which other birds migrate in Britain?
- Take poster paints – swallow colours are white, red and blue.
- A simpler version of the swallow can be made with clay for the body, leaves for the wings, and sticks for the tail and beak.

Swallow (*Hirundo rustica*)

Top tips

- This activity is most effective when the children are given as much context as possible in which to fire their imagination.
- Swallow migration usually occurs in March; this activity is best used then.
- Have extra wings and clay because many swallows won't complete the journey.
- At various stages on the journey, add incoming dangers such as a big storm or a hawk.

Invisible learning

- Migration awareness.
- Natural indicators – birds migrate because of changes in weather, seasons and food sources.
- Relationship and empathy with other species.
- Natural dangers for swallows.

Related activities

Nest robbers p.45   Birds activities pp.86–93

127

Painted beetles

How to

- Inspire children by looking at pictures of beetles or go on a quick insect hunt.
- Give each person a small amount of clay, about the size of a large marble, to mould into the main body of the beetle.
- Add small sticks and other foraged materials for legs, wings and pincers.
- Paint the clay beetles – poster paints work well.

Resources

- Pictures and books of insects
- Clay
- Foraged natural materials
- Paint

In spring, everything is renewed and refreshed. The flowers come out in vibrant colours and the bright green new leaves appear. It is a good time to think about insects, e.g. the beetles' colours being refreshed and made shiny.

Variations

- Find out about your beetle: what were its larvae like? What does it eat? How long does it live? What is its home like?
- When the beetles dry, varnish them to bring out the colours and make them lovely and shiny.
- Discuss how insects grow differently from mammals and plants – they have a hard outer shell (exoskeleton).
- Create a little home for your beetle.

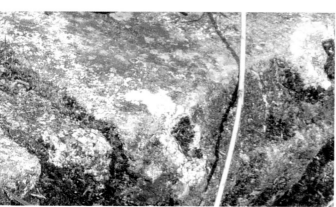

Top tips

- Avoid using too much water when painting.
- Bring extra clay, as beetles may well get lost in the forest.
- This activity was inspired by *The Story of the Root Children* (Sibylle von Olfers).

Invisible learning

- Empathy with creatures.
- Seasonal awareness.
- Basic classification.

Related activities

Beetle tag p.29   Bug hotel pp.94-95

Sticky-weed fun!

Sticky weed (*Galium aparine*)

Sticky weed, or cleavers, is a wondrous and abundant wild plant that is easy to recognise and has many fun uses. The juice or tea is an old and effective spring tonic, which helps to fight infection by clearing the lymphatic system.

130

Sticky-weed juice

- Introduce and identify sticky weed.

WARNING: Sticky weed in contact with skin can cause irritation or rashes for some people.

- Show how to gather it with the least possible impact. Make a tiny nest that can fit in the palm of your hand to be used as a sieve.
- Gather another handful of sticky weed to make into juice.
- Put the handful of sticky weed into a jug. Cover with cold water.
- Mash and squash the sticky weed with a clean stick until the water turns green.
- Strain the mixture into the second container using the sticky-weed sieve.
- Drink the yummy fresh juice.

Variations

- With younger children, make a communal jug of sticky-weed juice and pass it round the group so each child gets a go at mashing. Make a larger sieve to strain into the cups.

- Cut the mashing sticks from green hazel, which the children can peel as part of the activity.

- The juice is fresh and much like cucumber, but can be a little tickly on the throat. This can be helped (and sweetened) by the addition of apple juice.

- With older children, discuss the old country use of sticky weed as a sieve to strain milk in dairies and as a cleansing medicine to treat infection. The method of pounding in cold water comes from the physicians of Myddfai, an old lineage of herbalists in Wales.

Resources

- Sticky weed
- Containers
- Water
- Cut and peeled sticks
- Apple juice (optional)

Sticky-weed nests

- Late in spring when the sticky weed is long and strong, gather it carefully and wrap and mould it into nest shapes.

- These can be used for nest-building activities and as gathering vessels, e.g. for Easter eggs.

- Dried sticky weed from previous years is excellent for tinder bundles.

Sticky-weed crowns

- As with the nests, gather sticky weed late in spring and weave together to form crowns. The crowns can be the base on which to add spring flowers or be made into camouflage headdresses for hiding games.

A sticky-weed challenge

See if you can stick sticky weed to someone's clothes without them noticing!

Invisible learning

- Plant identification and uses.
- Herbal knowledge and ancestral history.
- Versatility of plants.

Related activities

Birds activities pp.86–93
Foraging wild plants pp.158-9   Fire lighting pp.178-9

131

Elderflower cordial

Elder (*Sambucus nigra*)

The elder tree is a magical and medicinal friend in the forest. The flowers herald the arrival of summer and the fresh cordial is a delight.

Beware: Positive identification of elderflowers is essential as there are poisonous lookalikes in the Umbellifer family.

How to

- Gather the creamiest, freshest elder blossoms on a sunny day. If you have a group of children, gather 2 flower heads each.
- Set up base camp and light a fire. Put 2 litres of water on to heat.
- Gather the group in a circle and destalk the flowers into a cup or bowl.
- Chop 4 to 6 lemons.
- Add elderflowers, lemons and 1kg sugar to boiling water.
- Place a lid on the pan and gently simmer for 20 to 30 minutes.
- If you have enough time, remove from the heat and allow to stand for 1 hour or so. If not, proceed straight to straining.

WARNING: Hot water and steam can burn.

- It is fun to strain the cordial through a sticky-weed sieve and this adds the medicinal properties of cleavers to the cordial (see p.130).
- Dilute and serve fresh elderflower cordial.

Resources

- Ingredients: 2 litres water, 4–6 lemons, 1kg sugar, lots of elderflowers
- Pan
- (Sticky-weed) sieve
- Measuring jug
- Bottles
- Cups
- Extra water to dilute

Variations

- Add other plants to the cordial – nettle tops and rose petals work well with elderflowers.
- Do a profile of the elder. It has compound umbels, pinnate leaves and a pithy core to the wood. Does it have poisonous lookalikes? How does it smell? The flowers are good for fevers, coughs and sunstroke: what other uses does elder have?
- Show how to sterilise glass bottles by steaming them, then pouring the boiling cordial in and sealing immediately.
- Make a bottles for each child and let everyone make a label for their own bottle.

Top tips

- Use organic or wax-free lemons.
- Keep the lid on while cooking over the fire to avoid an over-smoky flavour.
- Remove elder stalks, as they are slight irritants.
- Make a gift to the elder tree to say thank you.

Invisible learning

- Tree lore.
- Connection to seasons.
- Making medicine.

Related activities

Elder pencils pp.110-11   Woodland jewellery pp.112-13
Sticky-weed fun! pp.130-31   Fire lighting pp.178-79

Healing ointment

Plantain ointment is antibacterial and good for applying to minor cuts, bruises, burns, insect bites and nettle stings.

How to

- Light a fire.
- Gather 5 to 10 plantain leaves for each child. You can use ribwort and greater plantain (see foraging wild plants, p.158, for sustainable harvesting considerations).
- Wash the leaves and tear them leaves into tiny pieces into cups or bowls.
- Measure 1 small jar (40–50ml) of olive oil per person and then pour into the saucepan.
- Mix the broken leaves with the oil and put on the fire to warm.
- Cook the leaves gently, stirring regularly, for 10 to 20 minutes, or until the leaves look like they have lost their green vitality (which is now in the oil).
- While the plantain is infusing the oil, shave the beeswax. You will need approximately a third of a jar per person.
- Take the pan off the heat and sieve the mixture into a jug.

Ribwort plantain (*Plantago lanceolata*)

Discovering medicine in plants and learning to make a potion or cream is fascinating. Suddenly, you see medicinal plants everywhere and start to heal yourself!

- Wipe clean or wash the pan. Return the oil to the pan and add the beeswax shavings.
- While the beeswax is melting in the oil, prepare the jars by opening the lids and arranging them close by on a safe, flat surface.
- Once the beeswax has melted, carefully pour the ointment into the jars. Seal jars. Leave to cool and set.
- Each child can write their own label, which should include the plant's name, date and place gathered.

Resources

- Plantain leaves
- Clean water to wash leaves (plus extra to clean saucepan)
- Cups or bowls (one per child), knife and board)
- Small jar (40–50ml)
- Olive oil
- Saucepan
- Beeswax (pre-shaved or take a knife and board)
- Sieve
- Jug
- Labels and pens

Variations

- As you become more familiar with the seasonal plants that have healing properties, make them into ointments as well.

Top tips

- The ointment needs to cook gently, so be keep the fire burning low.
- Ask the children to tear the leaves into a cup. This helps them become familiar with the texture of the plant. Involve their other senses, too: crush the leaves between their fingers and smell or taste a small piece of plantain.

Invisible learning

- Plant lore.
- Survival skills.
- Sustainable harvesting.
- Teamwork.
- Integration of skills: foraging, fire making, measuring, cooking.
- Empowering self-confidence.

Related activity

Fire lighting pp.178-79

135

Walnut boats

Walnut (*Juglans regia*)

Sail your walnut boats in ponds, streams or puddles!

How to

- You need a collection of unbroken walnut shells. The best way to shell a walnut is to gently push the point of a knife into the darker, less-pointed end of the nut and twist. The kernel can then be removed and eaten. The shelling can comprise part of the activity.

- In the centre of the bowl of the empty shell, stick a small ball of beeswax, Plasticine or Blue tack. Insert a small stick as a mast.

- Pierce a small leaf on the mast as a sail.

- The little boats can be sailed on puddles or small ponds; you can also attach a cotton thread as a lead.

- Bring a spade and ask the children to dig a mini-lake, which can be lined with a large bin bag then filled with water.

- Have fun at the summer regatta!

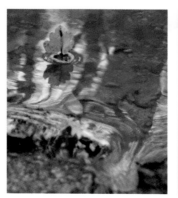

Resources

- Walnuts in their shells
- Knife
- Beeswax, Plasticine or Blue tack
- Cocktail sticks or sticks found in the woods
- Small leaves
- Cotton thread (optional)
- Spades or trowels for children
- 2 large bin bags (1 spare)
- Water

Variations

- Make little clay people to go in the boats.
- Create other boats out of natural materials in your environment, e.g. using bark.
- This activity is also good in the autumn, as it ties in with the nut-gathering season.
- Compare how different materials and objects of different weights and shapes float.

Top tips

- Keep walnut shells in a resource box to bring out when needed. It saves time and increases the flow of a session if they have been prepared beforehand.
- The masts sometimes fall off. If this happens, encourage the children to find small things in the environment to experiment floating in their boats.

Invisible learning

- Imaginative play: creating mini worlds.
- Volume and buoyancy.
- Natural resources.
- Hand-eye coordination.

Related activities

Flower fairies pp.108-9   Raft making pp.116-17
Hazelnut oven pp.190-91

Tree spirits

How to

- Give each participant a lump of clay.
- Choose a tree (or go to their tree if they have just played meet a tree, p.39) and create a face for the tree using the clay and anything they find in the environment.
- Take time for this activity. When finished, take a tour of the tree spirits.

Resources

- Clay (from the land or shop bought)
- Natural materials

Creating tree spirits brings the trees alive to children of all ages. This works especially well after playing meet a tree!

Top tips

- Ask a few questions like how the children think it might feel to be a tree. Or even questions that we cannot know the answer to, such as what has this tree seen in its life?
- If your local geology allows, it is easy to dig up your own clay.

Variations

- Make a tree spirit using clay and natural materials from a particular species, e.g. from the oak tree use its leaves, buds, twigs, flowers and acorns.
- Try taking a rubbing of the tree's bark.
- What is the tree's story? Imagine how long it has been there.

Invisible learning

- Nurtures creative expression.
- Empathy with trees.
- Discovering where clay comes from.

Related activities

Sit spot pp.92-93   Flower fairies pp.108-9

139

Waxed leaves

The colours of autumn are akin to those of fires and sunsets – take some home with you.

How to

- Gather many varieties of autumn leaves, press and dry them in books or a flower press. The leaves take a few days to dry. Either prepare this part in advance or see the gathering of the leaves as a separate activity.
- Light a fire. Melt beeswax in a pan over the fire.
- Take the pan off the fire and dip the leaves. To do so safely, hold the leaf stem and dip. Avoid immersing the fingers!
- Take the leaf out of the wax, hold above the pan and immediately shake downwards to remove extra wax before it dries. Avoid shaking side to side, as droplets of wax can go over clothing.
- Blow the leaves gently to complete the drying.
- The wax coating will help to preserve the leaves. They can be used for all sorts of crafts, and are especially lovely when threaded.

Resources

- Pressed autumn leaves
- Wax (beeswax recommended)
- Saucepan
- Needles and thread

Variations

- Link the activity with all sorts of leaf games and simple leaf fun, such as making big leaf piles and jumping in them, or trying to catch leaves falling in the breeze!
- Make mobiles with wax leaves and other autumnal natural objects.
- Make autumn leaf bunting.
- Just after removing the leaf from the melted wax, and while the wax is still warm, press the leaf on to clean jam jars to make beautiful lanterns.

Invisible learning

- Seasonal awareness.
- Brain pattern recognition of leaf shapes.
- Seeing the beauty in nature.
- Fire making, using natural resources and environmental art.

Top tips

- You need to manage the temperature of the wax and reheat it if it starts to cool too much.
- Thin, fragile leaves tend to curl and break.
- With younger children, hold their dipping hand with them.
- There is risk involved with children dipping leaves into hot wax. However, children focus and take a lot of care when given this responsibility.

Related activities

Plants and trees games pp.34–41
Clay gnomes pp.146-47   Fire lighting pp.178-79

Teasel hedgehogs

Teasel is a plant which has large flowers with spikes. It was used in the past for brushing cloth to give it a smooth surface.

How to

- This activity is best in a woodland setting, but can just as easily be done at home and in the garden.
- The hedgehogs are made with teasel heads and clay.
- Cut the teasel heads, leaving about 1cm of stalk, on which to attach the clay head. Trim off the long spikes at the base of the stem.
- Smear clay along one side of the flower head to form the hedgehog's belly, following the direction of the spikes to avoid being prickled.
- Form a cone-shaped head from the clay and push it onto the stalk.
- Mark eyes and noses with a sharp stick. Clay legs are optional.
- Create leafy shelters at the base of trees in which the hedgehogs can hibernate when winter is on its way and food is scarce. Discuss with the children how the animals will stay warm enough. Where is a safe place for them?

Resources

- Teasel heads (1 per child)
- Clay and sticks

Teasel
(*Dipsacus fullonum*)

Variations

- Repeat the activity in the spring, with a session on the animals coming out of hibernation.
- Create an animal profile on hedgehogs.
- This activity naturally leads to shelter building.
- Look at other native species that hibernate.
- Play a hibernating hedgehog game, where children bury each other in leaves and the fox tries to find them.
- Use a pine cone or a conker or sweet chestnut shell to make the hedgehog's body.

Top tips

- Discuss how we can protect hedgehogs hibernating in garden bonfire piles by searching thoroughly before lighting or waiting until spring.
- The teasel heads are full of seeds. Collect the seeds and either put them on the bird table (finches love them) or sprinkle them somewhere in your local environment, where they can provide future resources.

Hedgehog (*Erinaceus europaeus*)

Invisible learning

- Hibernation.
- Heritage species.
- Seasonal influences on wildlife.
- Relationship and empathy with other species.
- Shelter building.

Related activities

Bug hotel pp.94-95   Swallow migration pp.126-27

143

Nut and berry flapjacks

Autumn in the forest is the woodland harvest festival. Gather edible nuts and berries to create all sorts of delicious treats. The leaf-wrapping technique is an Indonesian method.

How to

- Gather (or buy) available nuts and berries, such as blackberries and hazelnuts.
- Light a fire and build it up so that there will be a nice big bed of embers.
- Shell the hazelnuts and chop or smash them into small chunks. Wash the blackberries.
- Mix the butter, sugar and oats together in a large bowl. Add the nuts and berries.
- Gather large non-toxic leaves, e.g. dock, sycamore or sweet chestnut.
- Demonstrate how to wrap the flapjack mix in leaves for cooking on the embers:
  - Lie a leaf on the ground in front of you.
  - With clean hands, mould some of the mix into a small patty and place in the middle of the leaf.
  - Fold the ends of the leaf over one another on top of the patty and stitch with a small stick or stem. Wrap another leaf around it in the opposite direction, so that all sides are enveloped, and stitch to secure.
- The children can now have a go at wrapping their own flapjacks in leaves.

- Rake the fire into a bed of embers and place the leaf-wrapped flapjacks on top.
- Depending on the heat of the embers, the flapjacks will need to be turned over after about 10 minutes. Total cooking time is approximately 20 minutes.
- Remove from the fire with tongs, allow to cool for 5 to 10 minutes, unwrap and enjoy!

Resources

(Makes 10–15 flapjacks)

- Berries
- Hazelnuts
- Pack of butter (250g)
- Brown sugar (250g)
- Rolled oats (400g)

- Large, non-toxic leaves
- Thin sticks for stitching leaves
- Bowl
- Spoon
- Spatulas or tongs

Variations

All sorts of food can be cooked in leaves in this way...

- Repeat the activity using different wild berries.
- A totally wild version of this can be prepared using acorns (although you must leach the bitter tannins to make edible); or chestnuts instead of oats, honey instead of sugar and animal fat instead of butter.

Top tips

- It can be easier to melt the butter and sugar first, although this involves using a pan.
- Wrap extra leaves around the flapjacks to prevent them from burning.
- Success lies in the heat of the embers and its even distribution.
- Keep a constant eye on the flapjacks and turn if the bottom leaf is blackening.

Invisible learning

- Wild cooking techniques.
- Native wild edibles.
- Preparing a fire for a specific purpose.

Related activities

Plants and trees games pp.34–41
Fire lighting pp.178–79   Wild food pp.186–193

Clay gnomes

In the autumn, seeds fall to the earth and the gnomes cover them with leafy blankets so that they can sleep through the winter and dream of what they will become in the spring.

How to

- Collect beautiful autumn leaves from the forest.
- Get a blob of clay that fits in the palm of your hand from which to shape the body. Mould the body with a flat base so that it can stand.
- Find a small stick, push it into the neck area, but leave some of the stick protruding. Roll another small ball of clay for the head and push it on to the top of the stick.
- Place a sheep's-wool beard underneath the chin.
- Use your fingers to shape the face and push in small beads as eyes or draw them on with a stick. Eyebrows and hair can be added.
- Add an autumn leaf cloak and hat. You can make the hat by twisting a leaf to make a cone and securing it with a stick stitch.
- Add ears.
- Go and find seeds in the forest with the gnomes. Plant the seeds and cover them with leafy blankets.

Resources

- Autumn leaves
- Clay and sticks
- Sheep's wool
- Little black beads (optional)

Variations

- When planting the seeds, discuss where the seed might like to grow. Use your imagination and ask your gnome what they think. Where will your seed get enough space and light?
- Use wax leaves for the gnomes' clothing.
- Extend the activity into a study of seed distribution or plant cycles.

Top tips

- This is a great activity for young children.
- If there are sheep grazing nearby, you are likely to find sheep's wool on a fence.
- Allow the children's imagination complete freedom in this activity – their creative ideas are often sources of surprise.
- Lichen makes good beards instead of sheep's wool.

Invisible learning

- The gnomes represent plant helpers and direct participation in awareness of the seasonal cycles of plants and trees.
- Nurtures creativity and imaginary play.

Related activities

Flower fairies pp.108-9
Waxed leaves pp.140-41
Fairy homes pp.168-69

147

Dutch oven bread

The smell of freshly baked bread makes everyone feel at home, especially in the woods. It is warming and comforting and requires a good fire, so makes for a great winter activity.

How to

- Prepare the dough in advance and allow it to rise prior to the session (especially in winter when temperatures are cold).

- This activity requires a good hot fire, lit early in the session to create a hot long-lasting bed of embers.

- Make a tripod:
  - Find 3 strong, straight sticks.
  - Tie them firmly together to make a tripod.
  - Make a hook from a branch – this is best cut green (live), otherwise it is in danger of catching fire.

- Spread out the fire so that when the Dutch oven is hung over it, there are only embers beneath. Flaming logs can cause the food to burn.

- Place the Dutch oven over the fire. When the pot has warmed up, place the bread inside. You can use a bread or cake tin that fits inside the Dutch oven, which can be raised off the bottom by sitting it on some evenly shaped stones.

- Replace the lid, hang it approximately 20 to 30cm above the embers. Use a spade to cover the lid with a thick layer of embers.

- Leave for approximately 30 minutes or until your instinct tells you it is ready. Use a fire glove to brush away the top embers. Blow off the remaining dust. A Dutch oven stays hot for some time, so take care!
- Fire-baked bread can be any number of shades on the outside, from black to light brown. When ready, it will have a hollow sound when you tap it with your knuckles.
- Cut on a chopping board and serve with butter.

Resources

- Bread dough
- 3 sticks and string or para cord for tripod
- Pruning saw (optional)
- Green branch
- Dutch oven
- Bread or cake tin
- Trowel or spade
- Fire gloves
- Knife
- Chopping board or plate to slice bread on
- Butter

Variations

- Cakes can be cooked in a caketin in the Dutch oven using the same method.
- Add seasonal flowers and wild edible berries, e.g. elderflower, blackberry or apple.
- The Dutch oven can be used for a huge variety of camp foods.

Invisible learning

- Cooking brings a feeling of being at home in nature.
- Preparation of fire for a specific purpose.
- Teamwork.
- Celebration and harvest.

Top tips

- Use seasoned hot burning wood, e.g. ash, beech, hornbeam.
- For a Christmas celebration, make the bread dough with plenty of raisins, cinnamon and honey – it is delicious and very festive.

Related activities

Foraging wild plants pp.158-9   Fire lighting pp.178-9

Snow shelters

Where there is plentiful snow and a group of willing hands, you can construct a life-size igloo in a couple of hours. To throw snowballs and build all sorts of sculptures and shelters is fun!

How to

- Choose a flat area of ground and mark a biggish circle with footprints. The igloo will stand here. The more perfect the circle, the stronger the igloo.
- Create blocks of snow that are similar sizes, making sure to tamp down the snow. Packing plastic boxes with snow works well.
- Put each block straight into place to form the first layer of your igloo wall.
- Build up the wall.
- From the third or fourth layer up, each block should overhang on the inside of the igloo by about 2 to 3cm. As the wall rises, the circles become smaller and smaller until they form the roof.
- While you can still climb over the wall, 2 people should stand inside the igloo. Their job is to receive blocks from people on the outside and lay them until there is only a hole in the top about 30 to 40cm in diameter.
- Cut out the door with a spade. Those in the igloo must stand away from where the door is being cut out. Once the cutting has been done, those on the inside can help push it out.
- The tallest person places the final block on the top to fill the hole. This block can be shaped with a spade to have slanting sides to fit the hole.

Resources

- Snow
- Large plastic containers, e.g. ice-cream tubs
- Spade

Variations

- Make a mini igloo sculpture by scaling down the method above.
- Have fun making a quinzee snow shelter. Use a spade to make a massive pile of uncompressed snow (2 to 3.5m). Hollow it out, but make sure you do not make the walls too thin by digging out too much. The walls should be about 30cm thick (you could measure this with a stick).

Top tips

- Do not put a snow block directly on top of the one below, but rather sit it across two of them just like the bricks of a house.
- Use extra handfuls of snow to seal the gaps between snow blocks.

Invisible learning

- Introduction to a shelter for cold climates.
- Understanding the self-supporting structure of igloo shelters.
- Working collaboratively to create something that would have been near impossible to do on your own.

Related activities

Tracking pp.96-97   Shelter pp.162–69

Evergreen wreath and crown

Holly (*Ilex aquifolium*)

This is a perfect winter activity for December. The children learn about native evergreen species while at the same time making a Christmas wreath. It is most suitable for a woodland environment where there is plenty of ivy.

How to

- The base of the wreath is best made with a circle of ivy woven around itself. Honeysuckle is also good, although better to harvest from the garden than wild sources.
- If the children wish to make a crown, first tie the ivy around their head with a simple overhand knot. Then each end is woven around the circle.
- Once the initial hoop is made, weave more ivy around it until there are enough secure gaps in the hoop for the children to add sprigs of other evergreens from the forest.
- Walk through the wood looking for and learning about the different evergreen plants and trees that grow there. Sprigs of these can be harvested with care and added to the crowns or wreaths.

Resources

- Secateurs
- Ivy or honeysuckle
- Natural materials

Variations

- It can be overwhelming to attempt to make individual wreaths or crowns in a large group. Instead, make one or two together, with everyone adding to them as you journey through the forest.

- Send the children on an evergreen scavenger hunt (see p.40) so they can bring back what they find to add to the wreaths or crowns.

Invisible learning

- Plant and tree identification.
- Plant and tree survival strategies.
- Native and non-native species in our environment.
- Celebration of continuing life, seasonal festivals.

Related activities

Plants and trees games pp.34–41
Sticky-weed fun! pp.130-31

Pyrite wands

All children love making magic wands. Here, we harness the magic of nature using primitive glue.

How to

- Find a suitable coppiced tree from which to cut a thin woody shoot – hazel, sweet chestnut and willow work well. Demonstrate and explain how to use tools safely with loppers, secateurs or pruning saw as appropriate (see Tool safety, pp.82-83).

- Choose a shoot, 2 to 3cm in diameter, for the wand and harvest with adult guidance and supervision.

- Continue to base camp and make a fire – children work together on the way to find and harvest dry sticks for a fire.

- Light a fire.

- To make the natural glue, heat beeswax and pine resin (ratio of 2:3, respectively) in a pan. When melted, add up to 1 part ground-up charcoal.

- Smear the resulting glue on to the end of the wand and add a small shard of iron pyrite. Dip the iron pyrite, base down, into the glue and squash it on top of the gluey end of the wand. Smear more glue around the base of the pyrite to ensure it is secure.

Resources

- Loppers or pruning saw
- Pan
- Beeswax
- Pine resin
- Charcoal
- Pyrite broken up into shards, or other local rock
- Water

Pyrite

Pyrite shards

Variations

- This activity ties in well with stories that involve magic and dragons. There is a saying, local to Sussex, that pyrite is the blood of dragons!
- The glue can be used for any number of activities.
- If pyrite is difficult to source, use another rock, more local to your area.
- The wands can be peeled or carved.

Top tips

- Make a few extra wands in case of breakages on the journey home.
- **Be careful when the glue is hot! Keep water to hand in case of burns.**
- To really secure the pyrite on to the wand, use string or wool to bind it to the wand and add glue on top.

Invisible learning

- Investigating where natural resources come from. Iron pyrite, pine resin and beeswax: mineral, plant and animal kingdoms.
- Geology of place.

Related activities

Looking after nature pp.18-21   Tool safety pp.82-83
Fire lighting pp.178-85

Primitive glue

155

Foraging wild plants p.158   Fire safety p.160

Shelter

Pages 162-169

- Shelter challenge
- Debris shelters
- Woven tipi shelter
- Fairy homes

Water

Pages 170–177

- Finding water in a landscape
- Water collection
- Water purification
- Water purification: boiling

Fire

Pages 178–185

- Fire lighting
- 10-minute fire challenge!
- Burn out a bowl
- Fire by friction: bow drill

Wild food

Pages 186–193

- Wild garlic pesto
- Hawthorn leather
- Hazelnut oven
- Wild food fritters

In the British Isles, we are fortunate to have such a rich, green natural world. The delicate balance of sun, rain and geology provides a perfect and varied habitat for a huge variety of plants and trees, each one with a myriad of intricate relationships to the world around them. Our ancestors intimately understood these relationships and knew which plants were good for food, medicine, making fire, baskets and clothing.

Discovering, harvesting and eating wild food is a fantastic activity. Connecting to our native food sources is educational, increases observational and sensory skills, and teaches different processes. As many as 40% of our modern medicines are derived from plants. Eating wild foods is also beneficial for our health because wild plants are so rich in the nutrients lacking in our refined modern diet.

Important considerations

- When harvesting be considerate and respectful: choose common, abundant species. Only take what you need and harvest a maximum of a third of the leaves.
- Always refer to a good plant identification book to positively identify a plant with total confidence before considering its ingestion.

Nettle (*Urtica dioica*)

- Research the plant's uses and cross reference from several sources until you feel certain of its identity and how to use it wisely.
- Learn all the deadly poisonous plants in your area. Does the plant you are studying have poisonous lookalikes?
- Consider pollution. Avoid gathering plants from roadsides, hedgerows by fields where chemical sprays are used, and waterways that might be contaminated.

Plums (*Prunus cerasifera*)

Ask questions such as...

- Which birds, insects and animals eat or live on this plant?
- Will I be taking too much of their food or habitat if I harvest here?
- Is there anything I could do for them in return?
- What is the leaf pattern?
- How many petals does it have?
- What kind of habitat does it thrive in?

Top tips

- Strike a balance between caution and confidence when trying new things.
- Children often like to thank the plant when harvesting. In this way, they develop respect for the living world.
- Use magnifying glasses to explore new species.
- Play plant games (see pp.34-41) and make wild teas (see pp.120-23).

159

Awareness around fires

- Only light a fire with the landowner's permission.
- In a group situation, it is a good idea to arrange seating at a safe distance from the main fire (about 1.5m).
- Before lighting the fire, check the direction of the wind and stand upwind of the fire. Avoid smoke inhalation.
- Do not light a fire in very dry conditions.
- A pair of fire gloves is useful, especially if cooking.
- Feed the fire with care.
- A stick in the fire stays in the fire.
- Keep your hair tied back if necessary.
- Always have water near your fire in case of any burns and to douse the ground and pour over the fire at the end.
- Follow the 'leave no trace' guidelines, p.20.
- Never leave a fire unattended.

Shelter challenge

A shelter helps you to stay comfortable and maintain a healthy body temperature. In Britain, an effective shelter is one that provides insulation, a windbreak and is waterproof. Life-size shelters take a good chunk of time to make well. Here are some fun, short challenges that help us to understand the principles of successful shelters.

Mini survival shelter

Sometimes we call these 'arm shelters' because we make them the size of your arm! It is a scaled-down version of a real survival shelter.

- Find a Y-shaped stick or branch. Stick it firmly into the ground. It will hold the main beam.
- For the 'backbone' of your shelter, choose a strong, straight stick about 30cm longer than your arm.
- Rest one end of the backbone in the Y-shaped stick, with the other end on the ground.

- Find straight sticks as 'ribs' for the shelter. Lean them against the backbone at about a 45° angle (photo A).

- Gather leaf litter to pile on to the structure to provide insulation by trapping pockets of air that your body heat warms up (photo B).
- Rather than sprinkling the leaves on, get an armful of leaves and use it almost like a brick. Start with the base layer, then build your way up to the top, layer by layer.
- Pack the inside of your shelter with the driest debris you can find. (The less air space you have, the warmer you will be.)
- Test the shelters: roll up your sleeves, put one arm in the shelter and one outside, wait 1 minute and note the difference.

Resources
- Dead sticks
- Leaf litter

Variations
- Make a shelter big enough to fit your head in that will be waterproof when tested. When made, use a jug of water to test the shelters – this is great fun, especially in summer weather! (Photo C)
- If you have time, make a shelter you can fit your whole body in (pp.164-165).

- Consider whether the shelters have been sited in a good place, whether they are pointing into the prevailing wind and whether there are any branches likely to blow down on them.

Invisible learning
- Hands-on understanding of how leaf litter works as insulation and could save lives in a survival situation.
- Teaches about structures, angles, and watershed.

Top tip
- If the 'ribs' slide down when putting them on, tilt them up a little towards the top end of the backbone stick and they should stay put.

Related activity

Water activities pp.170-177   Bug hotel pp.94-95

Debris shelters

The debris survival shelter uses the same style and principles as the mini survival shelters, but made life-size. Here, it is scaled up for a one-person survival shelter.

Debris shelter

- Take a good look at the mini survival shelter (see pp.162-63). We shall scale it up so that you can fit in!
- Location is critical (see top tips). Lie down to measure how big it needs to be.
- Find a strong Y-shaped stick and backbone and then start adding ribs.
- Once you have finished the ribs, add as much leaf litter as possible to insulate and waterproof the shelter. Save the driest debris to stuff inside to act as your insulation mat and sleeping bag.

Lean-to shelter

For simple group shelters, lean-tos are great. They are open-sided, pitched-roof structures.

- Locate the shelter away from hazards, near an abundance of good long sticks and leaves and ideally where trees can be used as supports for the main beam. If you are making just one lean-to shelter, face the open side away from the prevailing wind which comes from the south-west in Britain.
- Find a strong main beam, 10-15cm in diameter. Harvest either a green limb or a dead one that is not rotten.

- Secure the mainbeam horizontal, about adult waist height from the ground. Utilise either forks in trees or a few sturdy 'Y' sticks at either end as in the photo. Lashing may be necessary.

- Add ribs next. Get lots of long sticks as straight as possible. Line them up so they rest at approximately 45° against the main beam with minimal gaps between them.

- Gather plenty of leaves to cover your shelter. If you want it to be fully waterproof using just leaves, you may need to pile it up to over half a metre thick!

- The insulation value of a lean-to shelter is not nearly as high as a debris survival shelter. This is why a fire and a good stash of firewood may be needed in addition to your bedding.

- **WARNING: If you are going to have a fire next to a debris shelter of any sort, it could easily set alight like a giant tinder bundle! So take precautions – keep a full bucket of water nearby.**

Variations

- Try different insulation and waterproofing materials. How does grass work in contrast to leaf litter? Is a combination best?

Resources

- Strong dead sticks
- Leaf litter
- Tarp (helpful for transporting big piles of leaves)
- String to secure shelter structure

Top tips

- Square lashings are very helpful for securing the main beam of lean-to shelters to trees.

- Location is critical. Check for hazards, dead branches above, animal runs. You want well-drained soil, a flat and comfortable floor and resources close by.

- Building the leaf litter up from the bottom ensures a better covering rather than showering the leaves on.

Invisible learning

- Structures, angles, watershed, insulation.
- Teamwork.

Related activity

Fire activities pp.178-185

165

Woven tipi shelter

How to

- Find 8 strong sticks that create the height you need when leaning together at about a 60° angle.

- Once you have chosen where the centre of your tipi will be, work out where each stick will go. Use a piece of string radiating from the centre to check they are all the same distance from the centre.

- Take a shorter, strong stick with a pointed end and bang it into the ground with a mallet. Remove the stick to leave a hollow in which to insert each of the 8 sticks. Bring the sticks together at centre-top and lash them.

- Decide which two sticks will have the doorway between them. To help these take the extra strain of the doorway, insert a wooden peg in the ground just outside the tipi right next to these 2 sticks.

- Harvest flexible, straight green sticks – hazel or willow – to weave in and out of the main 8 sticks to form the walls. Depending on the scale of your tipi, you will need a lot of these!

- Leave a gap for the doorway and little gaps for windows.

If you keep returning to a certain spot, try an ongoing structure that introduces different building methods, tried and tested throughout our history. We spent several months adding to this woven tipi structure and then tried out some wattle and daub.

Wattle and daub

- A good daub is generally made up of binders (clay), aggregates (sand or crushed chalk), reinforcement materials (straw, hair or hay) and water. The binder holds the mix together. It is bulked out by the aggregate and the reinforcement gives it flexibility as well as holding it together as it dries and shrinks.

- Combine the clay with the water, aggregate and reinforcement material with bare feet on a tarp or builder's bag. Add the aggregates and reinforcement materials a little at a time until you have a consistency near to plaster.

- Slap it on to your wattled woven tipi and then smear it flat with your palm.

Resources

- 8 main poles and a wooden peg
- Flexible green sticks
- String
- Saw, mallet
- Secateurs or loppers
- Daub materials, e.g. clay, sand, water and straw
- Tarp or builders' bags

Variations

- Make traditional wattle-and-daub hurdles.
- Make a mini version of the structure. It is much quicker and you still experience the principles of woven structures and wattle and daub.
- Use green willow for your main 8 poles to create a living tipi structure, whose side branches you can weave into the structure over time.

Top tips

- Consider the time of year you are making the tipi. If you are harvesting many green sticks for weaving, it is kindest to the trees to do it in winter.

- If you are leaving a gap and need to weave a stick back on itself, twist it as you bend it to spread the tension over many fibres and reduce the likelihood of it snapping.

Related activity

Natural fibre cordage pp.102-03   Tree spirits p.138-39

Fairy homes

SURVIVAL SKILLS: Shelter

There is nothing better than a child's imaginative world of dens and homes for all!

How to

- Create a little creature using some clay and natural materials you find in the landscape, such as nuts, leaves, berries, sticks and feathers.
- Name your creature and have a little think about what kind of place it might like to live in.
- Find an area to create a home for your creature. Get ideas from the shelters on pages 162 to 167, or use your imagination and the natural surroundings to build the kind of home your creature would love.

Resources

- Clay
- Natural objects and materials
- Sticks and leaves

Variations

- Rather than inventing a creature of your own, make a clay model of a specific animal or insect. Learn what habitat they like to live in and recreate it for them.
- Create a home for the fairies or gnomes who may live in your area.
- Use natural objects and clay to make mini furniture, cups and plates, bowls full of food, etc., for whomever might live in the home you create.

Invisible learning

- Kinaesthetic exploration of natural materials and resources.
- Develops emotional literacy and storytelling skills through characterization.
- Learning through imaginative play.
- Trial and error about structures and habitats.
- Developing teamwork.

Top tips

- If some children find it challenging to engage with building a structure, either start making your own to give them ideas or help them get started by forming a simple backbone.
- Let their imaginations play freely.

Related activity

Flower fairies pp.108-09   Teasel hedgehogs pp.142-43

169

Finding water in a landscape

How to

- Consider where water always travels. What else is attracted to water that you might be able to follow? What plants or trees grow near water and may indicate a stream or area where the water table is close to the surface?
- Once you have established some ideas, you will start to look at the landscape through new eyes.

- Wander through the landscape with these thoughts in mind and go on a water hunt.

Water is vital to all life. The dynamic dance between the rain and the land brings abundance and well-being to us all; what a gift it is! A human can survive on average 3 days without water intake, but with serious consequences occurring along the way. A lack of water leads to dehydration, which affects individuals in the form of headaches, dizziness, confusion, lethargy and eventually death – not helpful when in a survival situation.

So, it is important to understand where to find water in a landscape and know how to make it safe to drink so you can stay well hydrated.

- Did walking downhill lead to a bog, stream or river? If you see deer tracks, consider where they go to drink. Where are rushes growing? Is the ground beneath them boggy? Is water near the surface? Where you see lines of willows, alders or birch, is there a stream or river they are growing along?

Resources

- Map of the area (optional)

Variations

- Draw a map of the landscape that you have walked and mark any water or species that indicate water is nearby.
- Have a good look at an OS map and model the landscape's contours from earth or clay. Use a watering can or plant sprayer to provide rain and watch how it flows over the hills and valleys. How does it erode the landscape over time?
- Look at a globe and see how water is distributed. Study different places in the world that have an abundance or scarcity of water and how it would be different to locate water in these habitats. Consider how different populations relate to water as a result of their ecosystem.

Invisible learning

- Importance of water as a survival priority.
- Flow of water in a landscape.
- Species that indicate water.
- Animal habits relating to water.

Top tip

- As a facilitator, scout out your water source in advance, either through a wander of the landscape or checking an OS map.

Related activity

Tracking pp.96-97

Water collection

The landscape provides clear channels such as rivers, streams, basins and ponds. There are many other less obvious sources of water to gather.

Dew collection

Dew collection is one of the most effective ways to collect water pure enough to drink from the immediate environment. Think how many times have you walked through a wet field and ended up with very wet trouser legs.

- If it is early and the grass is still dewy, or if it has been raining earlier in the day and you have access to a grassy area, have a 15-minute water collection challenge.
- Get into pairs or small groups.
- Give each group a bandana and a cup and send them off to see if they can fill their cup with rainwater or dew in 15 minutes or less.
- Drag the bandana through the wet grass to soak up the water, which can be wrung out in the cup.

Resources

- Bandanas
- Cups
- Water container
- Water
- Spade (for gypsy well)

Raindrops

One of the most magical and safe ways to drink in the wild is after or during a rain shower. Children love drinking the raindrops off the leaves of trees. Point out which leaves are safe and which should be avoided due to poisonous qualities. It can be an enchanting way to learn tree identification, to drink oak leaf droplets, silver birch water, etc.

Gypsy well

In boggy areas, when the water table is near the surface, you can dig a pit into the earth. This water source can be most easily found using indicator species such as alder and golden saxifrage. The principle of the Gypsy well is that the water that fills the pit has flowed through the earth and so is filtered on its way. Having been underground, it is more likely to be free of air-born or animal contaminants. Even so, it is always best to boil it to be on the safe side.

NOTE: see water hazards and purification on pages 170 to 177.

Invisible learning

- Understanding ways to meet our body's need for water in basic survival situations.

Top tips

- Consider the weather; water collection can easily lead to wet clothes, so this activity is best done in mild weather, unless you can warm up next to a good fire or head indoors soon after.
- It is great fun to pool the water everyone has collected and create a wild tea with it.

Related activities

Master tracker pp.53-54
Teas through the seasons pp.120-23

Water purification

Water hazards

We find ourselves in a time where our waters are polluted and in a survival situation; this really shows up and requires serious consideration of the following possible conditions:

- Biological contaminants from animal or human faeces can lead to such infections as cryptosporidium, giardia and E. coli, all of which can cause vomiting, cramps and diarrhoea.
- Bacteria such as leptospirosis from rat urine can lead to Weil's disease.
- Viruses, e.g. norovirus and hepatitis A.
- Chemical contaminants from agriculture.
- Heavy metals from industrial waste.
- Fly tipping.

In the following activities, use tap water, because invisible contaminants may be present, even in clear running water from our natural environment. The following processes are of great value as emergency survival techniques and as fun learning tools.

Drinking impure water can lead to major health problems that may continue for years and, at worst, can be fatal. Imagine a time when our ancestors freely drank from rivers and streams; let's hope that one day future generations will share that experience.

Water filtration

- Use layers of grass, charcoal, moss, rushes and sand to create a natural filter. Contain these layers in a plastic bottle with the bottom cut off, or in a sock. Another option in a survival situation would be to use a tube of bark with grass as the bottom layer.

- Discuss what qualities each of these materials may offer. Think about what order to layer the different-sized materials in order to filter the water.

- Try different combinations and discover what works best; you may need to pour the water through several times for best results. It will never come out totally clear, but compare it with what you started with.

- If you want to try drinking it, we recommend boiling it first – you could even make a wild tea.

Resources

- Old water bottles/socks
- Grass, charcoal, moss, rushes and sand.
- Cups
- Water container
- Drinking water

Invisible learning

- The need to filter water before boiling it.
- Hazards of drinking untreated wild water.
- Materials found in the wild that act as effective filters.

Top tip

- Use eyeglasses to look at the materials and explore why they make good filters.

Related activities

Looking after nature pp.18-21
Teas through the seasons pp.120-123

Water purification: boiling

Boiling challenge

- Get into small groups.
- Who can boil a cup of water the fastest?
- Give each group fire-lighting resources, a mug, some drinking water and a pot or kettle.
- Give clear boundaries about where to light the fires.

Resources

- Fire-lighting resources
- Mug
- Drinking water
- Pots or kettles

Variations

- Demonstrate making a tripod and hook, on which to hang your kettle.
- Boil water in a kelly kettle.

Once the water is filtered, it needs to be purified to ensure it doesn't contain any harmful bacteria or viruses. There are different ways to purify water, including purification tablets and boiling. Boiling is considered the most effective method for killing biological contaminants. Water must be boiled for at least 10 minutes for this to be achieved. It can be fun to practise water purification by boiling water over a fire in a pot or kettle. So, what do you do if you do not have a pot?

Wild boiling - hot rocks

- Collect rocks that are safe to heat (igneous). Avoid flint and river rocks, as these are prone to exploding and could cause injury.
- Make a fire and build up a good bed of embers.
- Heat the rocks in the fire for at least 40 minutes.
- Use a burned-out bowl (see pp.182-83) or other wooden bowl to put the water in.
- One by one, remove the rocks from the fire, dust off the ashes with a leaf brush and place in the water with care. It is best to use tongs.

Resources

- Igneous rocks (approximately golf-ball size)
- Burned-out bowl or wooden bowl
- Tongs
- Fire gloves

Hazard: Suitable rocks must be sourced for this activity. Do a practice run without young people to double check the rocks remain intact.

A lovely thing to do is to make solar infusions, sometimes known as sun tea! This simply involves adding an appropriate plant to a clear water bottle. The mint family, especially the aromatic ones, e.g. water mint and wild thyme, have strong antimicrobial properties. Delicious sun teas include sticky-weed, nettle and elderflower.

Invisible learning

- Gaining understanding of the need to purify water.
- Experiential learning about heat transfer.

Top tips

- Make sure you have a well-established fire before putting the rocks in to heat.
- Remind groups of the fire triangle: fuel, heat and oxygen (see p.178). It can be tempting to put the pot straight on the fire, as this might seem the hottest place, but this can put the fire out by restricting air flow.
- Sit the pot on trivets or large logs.

Related activities

Dutch oven bread pp.148-49
Fire activities pp.178-85

Fire lighting

There are many ways in which a fire can be lit, including matches, steel and striker, flint and iron pyrite, lightning, compressed air, friction, electricity, magnification, to name a few. For any fire to exist, though, there must be the right balance of fuel, oxygen and heat. This is called the fire triangle.

How to

■ Make charcloth prior to this activity by putting 100% cotton cloth into a tin with a tight-fitting lid. Pierce the lid twice and place the tin on the fire. Smoke will stream out of the holes; when it stops, remove it from the fire. Do not open until cool.

■ Create a tinder bundle – a nest of dry material, e.g. dried grasses, bracken, peeling-off silver-birch bark, reed mace fluff.

■ Gather all the materials needed to light a fire, from tinder to all grades of sticks.

■ Demonstrate how to create sparks from a fire striker in the air. Point out that the sparks are very hot when created but cool down quickly.

■ Show how to catch sparks on a piece of charcloth so there are glowing patches.

■ Give everybody a piece of charcloth in a shell or on a piece of bark and let them have a go.

■ When all have succeeded, gather their charcloth by tipping it off their shells into one tinder bundle.

■ Now blow it into flames.

■ When you have ignited the tinder bundle, place it on your prepared stick raft and gradually add sticks from thinnest to thickest to create a tipi structure.

■ Be aware as you are adding sticks to place them so there is always fuel above the heart of the fire, but not so much that it smothers it.

Resources

- Source of tinder, such as dry hay or bracken.
- Source of standing dead sticks of varying thicknesses from match-stick thin to thumb thick.
- Fire strikers
- Charcloth

Invisible learning

- Building a relationship with fire.
- Attention to detail and preparation.
- Understanding a process.
- Learning the fire triangle and how all three aspects are needed in balance.

Variations

- A group can get quicker success from replacing the charcloth with cotton wool, or even cotton wool dipped in Vaseline.
- Tinder bundle rumble: the challenge is to find materials in the natural environment that will make a good tinder bundle. Then put it to the test by taking a small ember from the fire, placing it in the bundle and trying to blow it into flames.

Top tips

- Always have the wind at your back when making fire to help avoid breathing in smoke.
- Make sure you have dead, dry sticks. Sticks on the ground may well have a lot of moisture in them. The best are standing dead wood (sticks that are dead but still attached to trees or caught up in them).
- Try the 'snap' test to see how dry the sticks are. The crisper the snap the better!

Related activities

10-minute fire challenge!

How to

- Set up an imagined scenario, where a friend has fallen into a lake in midwinter and if you do not get a fire going very soon, your friend will start getting hypothermia.
- The challenge is to get a small group fire going using natural resources from the immediate area in 10 minutes or less.
- Be clear about what resources are available to them. You may include in the scenario that one of the group has a handful of dry hay in a pocket and another has a box of matches, but with only 5 matches left.

Resources

- Source of ignition (matches or steel and striker)
- Source of tinder, such as dry hay or bracken. For the steel and striker, you may need charcloth or cotton wool
- Standing dead wood

It is good to keep developing your fire skills and testing yourself however adept you think you may be.

Variations

- Develop challenges such as lighting a fire to burn through a piece of string suspended above the fire, or to boil a kettle.
- Allow as much time as they need, but have the focus on good preparation and attention to detail by limiting their attempts to light the fire – the challenge being they only have 3 matches.

Invisible learning

- Refines fire-lighting skills.
- Learning through challenge, trial and error.
- Understanding fire-making materials and principles.

Top tips

- Have plenty of tinder available. It is likely that groups will need a few attempts and some guidance to achieve success.
- Allow more than 10 minutes to give opportunity for improvement.

Related activity

Teas through the seasons pp.120-23

Burn out a bowl

It is fun to have a purpose for lighting your fire. This may be cooking or boiling water for tea, but here are some other ideas of how you can craft using fire.

How to

- You need a well-tended fire.
- Harvest a bowl 'blank'. This will be a piece of well-seasoned wood from a tree that is non-toxic, e.g. birch, willow, sweet chestnut or poplar.
- Start with a flat surface so you can split a round piece of wood in half.
- Using wooden tongs or two sticks as chopsticks, take a hot, glowing ember out of the fire and place it on your bowl blank.
- While using a stick to hold your ember and stop it being blown away, blow on the ember to keep it hot. The heat from the ember will start burning into the seasoned wood.
- It is likely your ember will cool down or get too small, so change it for another one.
- The bowl blank itself will start forming embers. These are helpful and speed up the process.
- Keep doing this until you have burned in deep enough. Now scrape out the black and sand your bowl on the inside.
- Shape the outside as desired by whittling.

Resources

- Seasoned wood for bowl blanks and tools to process (saw, small axe or fixed-blade knife)
- Good firewood supply
- Tongs (optional)
- Bucket of water in case of burns
- Fire gloves

Variations

- Use the same principle to burn out a spoon bowl and whittle the spoon. Burn out a chamber for a long, thin boat.
- Use a large burned-out bowl to rock-boil water (see p.177).

Invisible learning

- Fire as a tool.
- Qualities of different woods.
- Carving skills.

Top tips

- When bowl burning, the fire needs tending, as everyone will take the hottest embers out of the fire, and this can leave it without a hot enough heart.
- Aim your breath at the point where the ember is in contact with the wood.
- If burning out a bowl, use seasoned wood. If doing a project like a spoon, where more whittling than burning is needed, it can be easier to use green wood but it is harder to burn out.
- Avoid flames because if the embers are alight while burning out your bowl, the bowl is more likely to crack. A short, sharp breath often puts out flames.

Related activities

Water purification: boiling pp.176-77
Fire lighting pp.178-79

Fire by friction: bow drill

There are many ways to make fire by rubbing sticks together, but they all use the same principles. Try rubbing your hands together really hard and fast. Can you feel the heat? It is caused by friction. When we apply this to sticks, they too get hot and create wood dust, which, if done right, will ignite!

How to

- There are 4 components to the bow drill kit: a hearth board, a spindle, a handhold and a bow with string on it.
- Harvest seasoned wood for the spindle and hearth board. Carve your spindle as straight and round as possible – about a hand-span long and as thick as your thumb. Sharpen both ends to a point.
- Carve your hearth board so that it is flat, as thick as your thumb and at least twice as wide as your spindle.
- Find a piece of bowed wood the length from your armpit to your finger tips.
- String the bow. It may take a few attempts to get the tension right, as you will need to twist the spindle into it, as shown.

- With the tip of your knife, twist a small hole into your hearth board, about 2.5cm from the edge, in which to sit the spindle.

- The handhold is a piece of wood that fits comfortably into your palm. Twist a small hole into the centre of it with a knife.
- Get in position: for right-handed people, that means having your left foot on the board next to your spindle with your left arm wrapped around the outside of your leg and wrist locked against your shin to steady the spindle. Have your knees at right angles. Place your right hand at the end of the bow.
- Place one end of the spindle into the hearth board hole and the other end into the handhold hole. Start by moving the bow back and forth, horizontal to the ground.
- Adjust speed and pressure as needed.
- Once you start getting smoke, keep going to burn in a socket that is as wide as the spindle.
- Carve in a notch. Imagine the black circle is a pie; remove a slice that is an 8th of the whole pie using your knife.
- Replace the spindle and continue bowing. If you are producing lots of smoke, keep going until your notch is full of dark dust. Carefully stop and remove the spindle. If the dust pile itself is smoking, this is an indication that you have an ember. Congratulations!
- Carefully transfer the ember into your prepared tinder bundle and light your fire.

Resources

- Seasoned wood of medium hardness
- Knife
- Strong string (para cord or shoelace)

Variations

- Try doing the bow drill in teams of 3.
- Try another friction fire method such as hand drill.

Invisible learning

- Patience.
- Perseverance.
- Principles of friction.
- Attention to detail.
- Refining a technique.

Top tips

- This is a skill that takes much perseverance and teaches many things along the way. Do not be disappointed if you don't achieve an ember.
- If you hear the kit squeaking, it is likely that you need more downward pressure.
- If your handhold smokes, lubricate (holly leaves, wax and soap work well).
- Good woods include poplar, hazel, lime, birch and cedar.

Related activities

Tool safety pp.82-83   Burn out a bowl pp.182-83

Wild garlic pesto

Wild garlic (*Allium ursinum*)

Pesto is a delicious way of eating a wide range of edible greens, such as wild garlic (also known as ramsons).

Caution: Positive identification of wild garlic is essential, as it could be confused with the poisonous leaves of lookalikes such as young lords and ladies (also known as arum lily).

How to

- Gather wild garlic. Wash and chop it.
- Blend using a mincer, adding nuts or seeds, salt and oil.
- Eat as a pâté on bread or crackers or serve with pasta.

Resources

- Chopping board and knife
- Mincer
- Oil (preferably olive oil)
- Sea salt, nuts or seeds
- Bread, crackers or pasta
- Bowl, knife, spoon, fork

Nettle (*Urtica dioica*)

Variations

■ Nettles, wild oregano, lime leaves, hawthorn leaves and sorrel are good wild foods to use in addition or as an alternative to wild garlic. Any wild edible greens can be used.

■ Use wild seasonal nuts and seeds, e.g. hazelnuts, instead of bought ones.

Invisible learning

■ Identifying leaf patterns.
■ Identifying edible species.
■ Recognising poisonous lookalikes

Top tips

■ For nettles, gather leaf tops in a bowl, then cut with scissors before mincing. By pressing and mixing the pesto for a while once minced, the sting of the raw nettle will be removed.

■ If you do not have wild garlic, use garlic from your garden or the shops. Lemon juice is good, too.

Related activities

Plants and trees games pp.34-41
Hazelnut oven pp.190-91

187

Hawthorn leather

Hawthorn is a small but noble tree of the British Isles that provides us generously with provisions through the growing season. The leaves, flowers and berries are all edible. The berry can be gathered easily and is fun to process. Here's one way.

How to

- Gather ripe berries (the larger and more tender the better).
- Destalk and remove any damaged berries.
- Wash and place in a large bowl.
- Add 1 cupful (or so) of boiling water.
- Stir the berries until the water is cool enough to handle then mash into a sticky pulp. For children, this is best done with their hands and is a fun task.
- Push the mixture through a sieve, thus removing the seeds.

- Spread the purée 2 to 3mm thick on a baking tray.
- In sunny, windy weather this can be dried outdoors, or else place it in a very low oven for 2 hours or so until the top of the leather is set. With a spatula, carefully peel it from the tray and either place it back in the oven until dry or hang it to dry outdoors or in the airing cupboard.
- It is vitally important to dry it completely or it will go mouldy. It can then be cut into strips or squares and eaten as snacks.

Resources

- Gathering basket or container
- Ripe Hawthorn berries
- Large bowl
- Water
- Spoon
- Sieve
- Baking tray, spatula, greaseproof paper

Hawthorn (*Crataegus monogyna*)

Variations

- Add other seasonal berries or fruits, e.g. blackberry and apple.
- Add honey.
- It also works with cold water.

Invisible learning

- Identification of seasonal, edible berries.
- Hand-eye coordination and sorting, i.e., berries from stalks and leaves.
- Plant processing.

Top tips

- Hawthorn is full of pectin, which sets well so can be included as a base for other fruit leathers made from seasonal fruits.
- Leave any pulpy seed remains out for animals and birds, or try planting them.
- This activity can include making a mat (see raft-making, pp.116-17) and use leaves instead of greaseproof paper. Use non-poisonous leaves, e.g. sweet chestnut.
- If left too long, the fruit leather can stick to its base or tray. Be sure to keep focused on the task and peel it off as soon as the top is dry enough.
- Discover more about hawthorn. Did people eat these berries in the Stone Age? What medicinal properties do these berries have? Do they make good jam?

Related activities

Hazelnut oven

How to

- Gather hazelnuts in September.
- Dig a shallow pit and line with sand.
- Place the nuts in a single layer up to 30cm or so in diameter.

- Cover the nuts with at least 1.5cm of sand.
- Light a fire on top of the pit and tend with sticks or split logs for about 45 minutes.
- Brush away the fire and uncover the nuts.
- Allow to cool before handling.
- Collect, crack open with nutcrackers or stones and enjoy the tasty kernels.

Our ancestors gathered hazelnuts in the autumn, placed them in shallow pits and roasted them. This way, the nuts are transformed into a delicious and far more digestible food for all the family to enjoy.

Hazel (*Corylus avellana*)

Resources

- Hazelnuts
- Spade or digging stick
- Sand
- Sticks or split logs
- Nutcrackers or stones

Variations

- Roast other seasonal nuts on the fire, e.g. sweet chestnuts. Make a cut with a knife in the skin before putting them on the embers.

Invisible learning

- Identifying edible nuts and seeds.
- Tree lore.
- Ancient cooking methods.
- Working with fire.

Top tips

- If it is difficult to transport sand to the site, this activity can be done directly in the earth, using the earth to cover the nuts.
- In order to reach the nuts before the squirrels, wait until the nuts look big and full on the trees and harvest them before they drop.
- It is interesting to look further into the archaeological history of cooking hazelnuts in this way. There have been digs on the Islands of Oronsay and Colonsay that show this was practised there *c.*7500 years ago.

Related activity

Fire lighting pp.178-79

Wild food fritters

How to

- Gather fresh edible greens or flowers.
- Wash and chop.
- Make a simple batter in a large jug.
- Add the greens to the batter.
- Heat the frying pan, add oil and pour in the mix.
- Flip the fritters and when cooked remove from the heat.
- Add salt or cheese, lemon or honey.

Making fritters on an open fire is one of the best ways to endear people to life outdoors! The smell of the sizzling batter in which freshly foraged greens imbue their medicine and flavours can tempt even the most cynical taste buds.

Resources

- Foraged greens or flowers
- Clean water to wash
- Chopping board and knife
- Large jug
- Batter ingredients: milk, eggs, flour
- Frying pan
- Oil or butter
- Spatula
- Lemon
- Honey
- Cheese

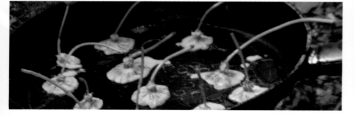

Variations

- Some favourite foraged plants for fritters include nettle, dandelion, sorrel and wild garlic.
- Use seasonal fruit, e.g. blackberries, elderberries or grated apple.

Invisible learning

- Identifying edible plants.
- Seasonal foraging.
- Making wild food accessible to the modern palate.

Top tips

- Some flowers can be cooked by holding the stalk, dipping in batter then cooking with the stalk up, e.g. elderflower and dandelion.
- Buckwheat flour is a great batter base and can be made with water and without eggs, making it vegan and gluten-free.

Related activities

Plants and trees games pp.34-41

In just a few generations, our relationship with nature in the developed world has shifted, from one of rich contact to one of complete disconnection. To witness true play in the natural world, unfettered by technology and gadgets, is uplifting and purely human.

One could say it serves human development on many levels, in particular on a spiritual plane, in a 'what makes us tick' kind of way. That is not to say we need to return to a Luddite existence; there is always a place for technology. This has been argued elegantly and eloquently by many writers, researchers, educators and philosophers over the years, from the romantics of Victorian times, such as William Wordsworth and John Ruskin, to contemporary writers such as Richard Louv and Richard Mabey!

Let's face it: the planet's ecological systems and the natural world communities ARE what make this small rock we travel on cosmically unique. If we are to survive and thrive, we need to reverse the 'breakdown' of these systems, communities

and human disconnection. Only through rich first-hand contact with the natural world can a love for and connection with these systems be invigorated in the human psyche.

This book gives us tools and stimuli to rediscover these deep connections in a joyful and life-affirming way. It helps people working with youngsters, in particular, to stimulate their natural curiosity. We all intrinsically have 'seeking' and 'play' systems in our emotional brains. Jaak Panksepp, sometimes referred to as today's Darwin of neuroscience, has shown these systems are hardwired into the mammalian brain, providing the basis for higher-order thinking in the human cortex.

Marina, Anna and Vicky have pulled together many proven and playful experiences in a tangible, attractive and very user-friendly way. This can only help learners reignite and progress these 'systems', and ultimately engender and develop the 'caring' system, also hardwired into our mammalian brains. It is these connections, enabled through playful, natural world 'whole body' experiences, that will allow individuals to play their part in cherishing and preserving the planet's natural systems, on which we all ultimately depend.

I recommend this book to you all – so get out, play and connect!

Jon Cree (Chair of the Forest School Association)

195

Marina Robb

Marina is founder and managing director of Circle of Life Rediscovery CIC, a leading outdoor learning organisation. Marina has been the recipient of funding from Natural England, Mind, and The National Lottery, among other grant makers for her outdoor work with teenagers, families and young people with mental health issues. She provides residential camps in Sussex woodlands, forest school and nature-based training for adults, outdoor-learning days and youth-training programmes.

A qualified teacher (PGCE), Marina has studied Environmental Education (MA), Environmental Management (BSc) and Social Research (MSc) since 1990. She is a leading forest school trainer and practitioner in the UK and abroad, and shares her knowledge and experience through training teachers and individuals who want to work outside the classroom. She is also trustee of SPARK, a network for young people's organisations in East Sussex.

Marina has spent her life supporting young people and adults to find new and old ways of connecting with nature and to reap the benefits of facilitated outdoor experiences. She is certified in Gestalt group facilitation, trained in wilderness skills, youth participation, managing challenging behaviour, non-directive play therapy and teenage psychology.

Marina's approach brings together best practice from environmental education, forest school, eco-psychology, indigenous wisdom and many years of working with young people of all ages and backgrounds, to create unique experiences. As a parent and workshop facilitator, she encourages young people to find their real voice, experience a sense of belonging and discover healthy pathways to adulthood.

www.circleofliferediscovery.com

Anna Richardson

Anna lives and works in East Sussex. A mother and a forest school facilitator and trainer, she works with people of all ages. A teacher of foraging workshops, Anna is enthusiastic about rediscovering the uses of wild plants and the indigenous approaches to sustainable harvesting for food, medicine and other practical crafts.

Over the last 20 years, Anna's interest in plants and traditional skills has developed through training, teaching and practicing bushcraft and through studying Plant spirit medicine with Eliot Cowan. Also through invaluble time spent in the field with Gordon Hillman, Professor of Archaeobotany at University College London. Anna has taught a course entitled 'Wild Plants and their Ancient Uses' at the University of Sussex CCE (in connection with the archaeology department), and continues to develop her own knowledge and inspiring ways to teach plantlore alongside a love for the natural world.

Passionate about new and indigenous ways to educate, Anna co-creates local community projects that enable people to share and learn together to reconnect with nature. She also enjoys the creative arts, plays fiddle and is actively involved in running folk-music sessions in the local area.

Victoria Mew

Victoria has followed her love of nature and curiosity in indigenous cultures since she was 12 years old, when she was introduced to a wilderness family camp and slept out in a lean-to shelter with a fire for the first time. Throughout her teens, she pursued this interest, training with Trackways, Coyote Tracks and the Tracker School.

Victoria has developed her skills in nature, sensory awareness, primitive living and wilderness philosophy. She trained with Wilderness Awareness School, WA, USA, building up experiences that culminated in a week-long survival quest in the Cascade Range mountains, where she tracked coyotes until she caught up with them, learned what wild plants could be harvested for a meal, experimented with different types of shelters, and was mentored on how to bring these skills to children of all ages.

She gained a BSc in Human Sciences at University College London, where her dissertation explored how growing up separate from natural environments affects childhood development. She has since founded Cultivating Curiosity, an organisation that works with people of all ages outdoors facilitating deep nature connection. She is also a qualified forest school practitioner.

www.cultivating-curiosity.co.uk

Resources

We aim to use natural resources rather than shop-bought items, but some purchases support certain activities. For tools and field guides we recommend www.greenmanbushcraft.co.uk and www.muddyfaces.co.uk; for clay, we use www.heskethps.co.uk. Some resources inevitably work out to be more affordable from such websites as eBay or Amazon.

Further reading

Outdoor play

Bentley, T., *Learning Beyond the Classroom: Education for a Changing World*, London: Routledge, London, 1998

Bilton, H., *Playing Outside: Activities, Ideas and Inspiration for the Early Years*, Routledge, London, 2005

Bruce, T., *Learning through Play: For Babies, Toddlers and Young Children*, 2nd ed., Hodder Education, London, 2011

Bruce, T., *Time to Play in Early Childhood Education*, Hodder Education, London, 1991

Garrick, R., *Playing Outdoors in the Early Years*, 2nd ed., Continuum, London, 2009

Guldberg, H., *Reclaiming Childhood: Freedom and Play in an Age of Fear*, Routledge, 2009

Tovey, H., *Playing Outdoors: Spaces and Places, Risk and Challenge*, Open University Press, Maidenhead, UK, 2007

White, J., *Playing and Learning Outdoors: Making Provision for High-Quality Experiences in the Outdoor Environment*, Routledge, London, 2007

Forest school, nature and environmental education

Disinger, J. F., 'The Purpose of Environmental Education: Perspectives of Teachers, Governmental Agencies, NGOs, Professional Societies, and Advocacy Groups', in Johnson, E. and Mappin, M., *Environmental Education and Advocacy: Changing Perspectives of Ecology and Education*, Cambridge University Press, Cambridge

Elpel, Thomas J., *Participating in Nature: Wilderness Survival and Primitive Living Skills*, HOPS Press, Montana, 2009

Knight S., *Forest School for All*, Sage Publications, London, 2011

Maynard, T., 'Forest Schools in Great Britain: An Initial Exploration', *Contemporary Issues in Early Childhood*, vol. 8, no. 4, 2007, pp 320–30

Palmer, J. and Neal, P., *The Handbook of Environmental Education*, Routledge, London, 1994

Swarbrick, N., Eastwood, G. and Tutton, K., 'Self-esteem and Successful Interaction as Part of the Forest School Project', *Support for Learning*, vol. 19, no. 3, pp 142–46

Vare, P. and Scott W., 'Learning for a Change: Exploring the relationship between education and sustainable development', *Journal of Education for Sustainable Development*, vol. 1, no. 2, pp 191–98

Learning and development

Claxton, G., *Building Learning Power*, TLO, Bristol, 2002

Gill, T., *No Fear: Growing Up in a Risk Averse Society*, Calouste Gulbenkian Foundation, London, 2007

Goleman, D., *Emotional Intelligence: Why it Can Matter More than IQ*, Bloomsbury, London, 1996

Kolb, D. A., *Experiential Learning: Experience as the Source of Learning and Development*, http://academic.regis.edu/ed205/Kolb.pdf

Lindenfield G., *Confident Children: Help Children Feel Good about Themselves*, Harper Collins, London, 1994

Pound, L., *How Children Learn, Step Forward Publishing*, London, 2005

Practical

Bang, P. and Dahlstrom, P., *Animal Tracks and Signs*, Oxford University Press, Oxford, 2001

Bruton-Seal, J. and Seal, M., *Hedgerow Medicine: Harvest and Make Your Own Herbal Remedies*, Merlin Unwin Books, Shropshire, 2008

Cornell, J., *Sharing Nature with Children: The Classic Parents' and Teachers' Nature Awareness Guidebook*, Dawn Publications, Nevada City, 1999

Hofmann, H., *Wild Animals of Britain and Europe*, Collins, London, 1995

Johnson, O. and More, D., Tree Guide, Collins, London, 2004

Kochanski, M., Bushcraft: *Outdoor Skills and Wilderness Survival*, Lone Pine Publishing, Washington, 1987

Mabey, R., *Food for Free*, Collins, London, 2007

Mears, R., *The Complete Outdoor Handbook*, Rider & Co, London, 1992

Montgomery, D., *Native American Crafts & Skills*, The Lyons Press, Connecticut, 2000

Olsen, L.H., Sunesen, J. and Pedersen, B.V., *Small Woodland Creatures*, Oxford University Press, Oxford, 2001

Phillips, R., *Wild Flowers of Britain*, Pan Books, London, 1977

RSPB Pocket Nature Wildlife of Britain, Dorling Kindersley, London, 2009

Smith, A., *Accelerated Learning in the Classroom*, Network Educational Press Ltd, Staffordshire, 1996

Sterry, P., *British Wildlife*, Collins, London, 2008

Other

Cornell, J., *Sharing Nature with Children II*, Dawn Publications, California, 1999

Cowan, E., *Plant Spirit Medicine*, Swan-Raven, North Carolina, 2007

Holland, C., *I love my World*, Wholeland Press, Dorset, 2009

Louv, R., *Last Child in the Woods: Saving our Children from Nature-Deficit Disorder*, Atlantic Books, London, 2010

Schofield, J., and Danks, F., *Go Wild! 101 Things to do Outdoors Before You Grow Up*, Frances Lincoln, London, 2009

Smith, L. T., *Decolonizing Methodologies: Research and Indigenous Peoples*, Zed Books, London, 1999

Van Matre, S., *Earth Education: A New Beginning*, Institute for Earth Education, West Virginia, 1990

Wade, K., 'Environmental Education in In-service Education: The Need for New Perspectives', *Journal of Environmental Education*, vol. 27, no. 2, pp 11–17

Warden, C., *Nurture through Nature*, Mindstretchers, Perthshire, 2007

Young, J., Haas, E., and McGown E., *Coyote's Guide to Connecting with Nature*, Washington: OWLink Media

8 shields
CA, USA
W: www.8shields.com
E: contact@8shields.org

Children of the Earth Foundation
NJ, USA
T: +1 609 971 1799
W: www.cotef.org
E: info@cotef.org

Circle of Life Rediscovery CIC
East Sussex, UK
T: +44 (0)1273 814 226
W: www.circleofliferediscovery.com
E: info@circleofliferediscovery.com

Corvus: Natur-und Wildnisschule Bodensee
Friedrichshafen, Germany
T: +49 (0)7553 2 463 362
W: www.corvus-bodensee.de
E: info@corvus-bodensee.de

Cultivating Curiosity
West Sussex, UK
T: +44 (0)7540 617 851
W: www.cultivating-curiosity.co.uk
E: info@cultivating-curiosity.co.uk

Forest School Association
Cumbria, UK
T: +44 (0)1228 564 407
W: www.forestschoolassociation.org
E: enquiries@forestschoolassociation.org

Ghost River Rediscovery
AB, Canada
+1 403 270 9351
W: www.ghostriverrediscovery.com
E: SRoss@ghostriverrediscovery.com

Institute for Outdoor Learning
Cumbria, UK
T: +44 (0)1228 564 580
W: www.outdoor-learning.org
E: institute@outdoor-learning.org

Man Among the Helpers
AZ, USA
W: www.manamongthehelpers.com
E: sal@manamongthehelpers.com

National Trust
South Yorkshire, UK
T: +44 (0)844 800 1895
W: www.nationaltrust.org.uk
E: enquiries@nationaltrust.org.uk

Natur & Wildnisschule der Alpen
Tirol, Austria
T: +43 (0)5 12 54 60 31
W: www.wildniszentrum.at
E: office@wildniszentrum.at

Nature Culture Foundation
T: +44 (0)7966 514 469
W: www.natureculturefoundation.com
E: info@natureculturefoundation.com

Natural England
South Yorkshire, UK
T: +44 (0)300 600 3900
W: www.naturalengland.org.uk
E: enquiries@naturalengland.org.uk

Play England
London, UK
T: +44 (0)20 7843 6300
W: www.playengland.org.uk
E: playengland@ncb.org.uk

Project Wild Thing
W: www.projectwildthing.com
E: hello@greenlions.com

Royal Society for the Protection of Birds
Bedfordshire, UK
T: +44 (0)1767 693 690
W: www.rspb.org.uk

Wilderness Awareness School,
WA, USA
T: +1 425 788 1301
W: www.wildernessawareness.org

Wilderness Foundation
Essex, UK
T: +44 (0)207 183 0689
W: www.wildernessfoundation.org.uk
E: info@wildernessfoundation.org.uk

Wildlife Trusts
Nottinghamshire, UK
T: +44 (0)1636 677 711
W: www.wildlifetrusts.org
E: enquiry@wildlifetrusts.org

Photograph credits

The authors and publisher would like to thank the following individuals for permission to reproduce images in this book. In all cases, every effort has been made to credit the copyright holders, but should there be any omissions or errors the publisher would be pleased to insert the appropriate acknowledgement in any subsequent edition of this book. All images are courtesy of and copyright the authors unless otherwise stated below.

L = left; R = right; T = top; B = bottom; C = centre

© Will Heap, photographer: front cover, 19L, 19C, 19R, 78–79, 84–85, 159R, 170L, 170–71B

© Gordon Hillman, archaeo-botanist: 121TL, 121BL, 121R, 122TR, 123L, 124C, 130L, 132L, 134L, 142C, 158–59, 159TL, 159BL, 187TR, 188L, 188CT, 188CB, 190L

© Susan Kelly, teacher, illustrator: 13, 14, 57C, 57R, 89TR, 162L

© Ameliee Collins, parent: 95BR

© David Clare, grandparent: 11R

© Dhyanna Miller, nature mentor: 87TR, 92TR, 92–93CB

© Julie Ruse, photographer: 5, 9, 15TR, 194–95, 208

Vladimir Salman © 123RF.com : 29BR

Michael Lane © 123RF.com : 30BR, 45BR, 48BR, 52C, 55R, 76B, 85L, 85CR, 93R, 127TR, 143R

Khursaini A Fatah © 123RF.com : 31R

Anna Wnuk © 123RF.com : 32TR

Stanislav Duben © 123RF.com : 43R

Richard Thomas © 123RF.com : 46R

Ken Liu © 123RF.com : 49BR

Rudmer Zwerver © 123RF.com : 50B

Lorna Roberts © 123RF.com : 51B

Jacek Cudak © 123RF.com : 54TR

Patthanapong Watthananonkit © 123RF.com : 54BR

Megan Lorenz © 123RF.com : 58BR

Guy Sagi © 123RF.com : 59BR

colette2 © 123RF.com : 63BR

stephan morris © 123RF.com : 65R

Mark Bond © 123RF.com : 85CL

Andrew Lever © 123RF.com : 85R

alucard21 © 123RF.com : 97R

13625197- Vadim Naumenko © 123RF.com : 121TR, 124L

Igor Golovnov © 123RF.com : 122L

Andrey Khrobostov © 123RF.com : 122BR

renegade photography © 123RF.com : 152L

Sandra Matic © 123RF.com : 191TL

Entries in **bold** refer to activities and their variations; numbers in *italic* refer to photographs

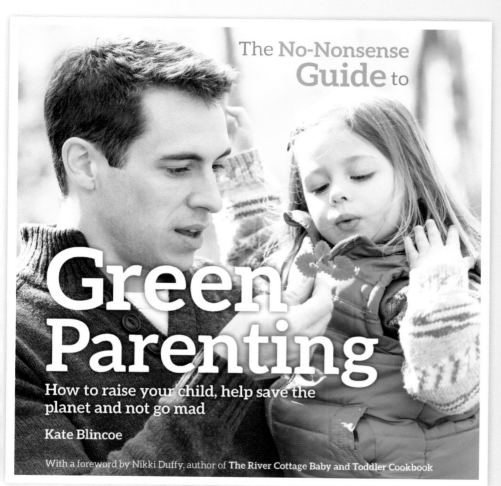

The No-Nonsense Guide to Green Parenting
Guide to

Green Parenting

How to raise your child, help save the planet and not go mad

Kate Blincoe

With a foreword by Nikki Duffy, author of **The River Cottage Baby and Toddler Cookbook**

The No-Nonsense Guide to Green Parenting: how to raise your child and save the planet

Kate Blincoe

A practical and down-to-earth guide to raising children in an environmentally friendly way, *The No-Nonsense Guide to Green Parenting* is the book that every eco-minded parent needs. Aimed at parents of zero to ten year olds, this book will help you live a greener lifestyle while still being pragmatic about raising your family.

The book is filled with helpful information and ideas. It will inspire you to explore nature, have fun together outside, and make decisions around the home that are both ecological and money saving. Maintaining your environmental values and embracing nature is not about being perfect – it's about giving it a try and feeling the benefits for your family.